WHEN TI
INVADE THE CANCER
CONQUEROR

SOLITARY KIDNEY AND NO LYMPH NODE, PROSTATE, OR BLADDER

WHEN THOUGHTS INVADE THE CANCER CONQUEROR

SOLITARY KIDNEY AND NO LYMPH NODE, PROSTATE, OR BLADDER

S NILAKANTA SIVA AND RAJALAKSHMI SIVA

Notion Press

Old No. 38, New No. 6

McNichols Road, Chetpet

Chennai - 600 031

First Published by Notion Press 2016

Copyright © S Nilakanta Siva and Rajalakshmi Siva 2016

All Rights Reserved.

ISBN 978-93-5206-931-6

When the eyes dim with age, spectacles come into the picture. When one gets hard of hearing, the hearing aids take control. When the teeth refuse to mash and grind, dentures come to the rescue. When the hands or the legs get disfigured, prosthetic legs from Jaipur lend support. Then why should urostomy bags, used when the urinary system malfunctions, make you feel like an odd one out?

— Nilakanta Siva and Rajalakshmi Siva

This book is dedicated to my father, the late Mr N S Siva (born 1916) in his centenary year.

My father always said that my idiosyncrasies and stubborn ignorance were enough to write a book. But the results of my smoking addiction was the real trigger in the creation of this book.

There would have been only about half the number of cases of bladder cancer if only we had listened to our parents' advice to quit smoking when we were teenagers in the 1960s.

Nilakanta Siva & Rajalakshmi Siva

DISCLAIMER

This book is based on real life experiences. Names have been changed for the sake of anonymity.

This book is neither a substitute for the medical advice of physicians nor a reference book for medical students. The surgery descriptions in the book reflect the author's perception of what happened. In the process of enhancing the plot's drama, certain inaccuracies and exaggerations may have inadvertently crept in. **In case of doubt or inaccuracy, students should let their mentor's modus operandi overrule the descriptions in the book.** *The reader should consult a physician immediately on finding any signs and symptoms that may require medical attention.*

This book is particularly targeted at smokers to warn them of the consequences of their habit.

CONTENTS

ACKNOWLEDGEMENT

Forever in grateful appreciation of:

❖ **our nephews**, Dr Prakash and Dr Sathish, who advised rapid follow-up on the episode of gross hematuria

❖ **our family members**, including our siblings and their spouses, our sons and their wives, and our cousins and their families for giving us sustained moral and physical support

❖ **our uro-oncologist**, Dr N Ragavan, who led the team of doctors through several ups and downs to finally succeed in the war against cancer

❖ the **several doctors** who followed our story on **Facebook**, right from the time it was conceived to its current state, as the book took shape week on week, and ensured that there were no serious medical blunders

❖ and the ever-enthusiastic **publishing team** without whose tireless efforts our thoughts would have never seen the light of day.

SYNOPSIS

Cancer has always been viewed as a parasitic monster that eats away at one's insides, silently and stealthily, till one reaches a point of no return. Many obituaries talk about people who "battled valiantly, but to no avail." And once in a blue moon, one hears of those who survived the onslaught of cancer. The word 'survival' is a misnomer, as these people did not manage to just scrape through alive; they fought all the way till the end and succeeded in defeating cancer.

In this book *When Thoughts Invade the Cancer Conqueror*, Kuppuswamy talks about his addiction to smoking during his college days and how he gave up the habit once his two boys became teenagers. Unfortunately, his crime from the past meets with a punishment. There are no mercy petitions for a crime as heinous as smoking and the long-term price must be paid. Bladder cancer caught up with him on his seventieth birthday when it revealed its presence in the form of hematuria. In fact, it was a bit of urine in a pool of blood. After several bouts of surgery, some comfortable, some painful and some downright irksome, the details of which are vividly described in successive chapters, Kuppuswamy conquered cancer. Faced with several irrational fears and a few premature celebrations, the treatment was one hell of a roller coaster ride. It was an emotionally draining time for Kuppuswamy and his wife Pramila.

With the team of doctors leaving no stone unturned, every medical specialty under the sun—oncology, nephrology, urology, anaesthesiology, cardiology, neurology and interventional radiology—came to the fore. Every possible medical expert and consultant, including the physiotherapist, had a role to play in his rapid recovery and rehabilitation. Only the orthopaedic and the psychiatrist were perhaps missing.

Hundreds of doctor friends interacted with him on Facebook and kept his spirits alive. Kuppuswamy's recovery and rehabilitation was like a dream-come-true for the team of doctors working on him. All the doctors were younger than his own children. Thankful to the new lease of life, Kuppuswamy began to counsel cancer patients.

How Kuppuswamy, his family and his near and dear won the war on cancer forms the crux of this story.

An important question here is this:

Would you rather be dead with all your organs in place or live with your kidney legated, bladder bagged and prostate in a basket?

The answer is it does not matter what the surgery takes away from you, what matters is how well what remains is functioning.

Life without a bladder, prostate and several lymph nodes is not all that bad.

When the eyes dim with age, spectacles come to the fore. When one gets hard of hearing, the hearing aids take control. When the teeth refuse to mash, dentures come to the rescue. When the legs are disfigured, Jaipuri legs lend support. When none of the above cause any embarrassment, why should ostomy bags, used when the excretory system malfunctions, make you feel like an odd one out?

CHAPTER 1
THE GENESIS

The root of all suffering

It was a little more than fifty years ago. Kuppuswamy was in one of the best colleges in town studying in the first year of intermediate class. He had done his schooling at a premier school and had been a regional topper at the General Certificate of Education examinations of the Cambridge University's Local Examinations Syndicate, commonly referred to as the Senior Cambridge exam. He was a studious student but botany and zoology were not his cup of tea.

Kuppuswamy's father was a senior IAS (Indian Administrative Service) officer posted in a metropolitan city. He hoped his son would be the first doctor in the family. In those days, the medical profession had an enormous charm and allure; medical practitioners were highly respected members of society. There had been no real doctor in the family. One grandfather had been a homeopath and that was all. The other grandfather had served in the royal Indian Police Service.

But Kuppuswamy could not sketch even the parts of a leaf or a butterfly or the transverse section of a frog in his biology laboratory record book. The mere sight of an earthworm or a lizard made him squirm. He was unable to differentiate a rose from a lotus, forget mastering the family, genus and phylum of the plant world or the animal kingdom. Every time he looked into the microscope, he felt as though he was putting his head into the jaws of a lion. It didn't seem as though he would get past even the first year in college.

Hardcore academics was down the pecking order of his priority list. Cricket was his first and only passion.

Kuppuswamy had represented his school at the inter-school cricket championship. He was aiming to get into the college team and, hopefully, the university team too. The ground where club cricket matches were held was just across the street from his house. The great and the not so great batsmen such as Gavaskar, Kambli and Amre frequently played here.

"Hey Kuppuswamy, you know what? They are calling for volunteers to join the National Cadet Corps (NCC)," screamed Vivek, his best friend.

"With a body weight of forty kilograms and a height of barely five feet two inches, no one would even let me sign up for NCC," remarked Kuppuswamy.

"They are short of the required numbers to form the battalion. They will definitely take in anyone who is prepared to don the *khaki* uniform and join the parades regularly. You will learn how to handle a .303 rifle at the firing range," Vivek continued.

"Wow. That sounds interesting."

"And that is not all. You get credits for all the hours you spend at NCC and the annual social service camp in summer. So you need not attend biology classes. You are totally exempt from them. Of course, studying medicine will no longer be an option for you. As for me, I can bunk the migraine-inducing mathematics classes."

"That is great. Long live NCC and the credit system," they shouted in unison.

While this meant Kuppuswamy's dream of playing professional cricket took a backseat, it was too hard to resist the thought of skipping botany and zoology classes. And learning to handle a firearm was a thrilling proposition.

The NCC sessions were not only for the new recruits but also for the senior cadets and officer-rank students. At the training, Kuppuswamy was in the midst of army personnel and commanding officers. He really enjoyed the parade and the military style training. During the interval, *vada-pav* and tea were served. Kuppuswamy really looked forward to the break, in which groups of men huddled together to light up cigarettes.

No one at home had any clue to what was happening. Suddenly, Kuppuswamy started skipping lunch, although he took money for lunch every day. He saved a lot of money by not eating anything through the day, apart from some junk food. He left home early in the morning and came home very late in the evening. He saved bus fare by walking half the distance to college and back home too. By the time he got home in the evening, he was famished beyond words.

And in a marked departure from his usual self, Kuppuswamy was suddenly so eager to run errands and buy grocery and other things for the house.

People wondered what had come over Kuppuswamy. They were puzzled but not for too long. In a few months, it became clear that he was saving money to buy cigarettes. He had joined one of the groups in college that spent all free time and money smoking.

Kuppuswamy's friend had a tiny crush on him. She had studied with him for eleven years in school. When she came to know that Kuppuswamy was puffing smoke like a steam engine, she was taken aback. She confronted him. But Kuppuswamy managed to convince her that since the cigarette he smoked had a filter at one end, his lungs would not get charred. She did not want to ask him anything more. In those days, lung cancer was the only known risk from smoking. Little did Kuppuswamy know that this casual habit would manifest itself as gross hematuria (plenty of blood in the urine) fifty years later.

Later, subsequently, while in the hostel at IIT (Indian Institute of Technology), Kuppuswamy had unfettered access to cigarettes. He could smoke whenever and wherever he wanted to, except in the classrooms and the laboratories. Though Kuppuswamy was now more aware and informed of the dangers of smoking than before, he couldn't stop himself from smoking. He was now strongly addicted to it. The writing on the wall was clear. It was only a matter of time before he would be diagnosed with cancer of the bladder.

It is now well-known that cigarette smoke contains high levels of several cancer-causing agents. While some act locally, others impact distant cells causing damage at the genetic level. Some of the auto repair mechanisms of the body are affected too. Abnormal cells are formed throughout one's lifetime and these are corrected by the body's inherent systems. However, aging and undesirable lifestyles (tobacco smoking in particular) put these mechanisms out of commission.

When smoke is inhaled, toxic chemicals pass into the bloodstream from the lungs. Blood then flows through the kidneys; the carcinogens end up concentrated in the urine. While the urine remains in the bladder, the toxins damage cells in the bladder lining, causing bladder cancer over a long period of time. There is a widespread misconception that drinking plenty of fluids and frequent voiding of the bladder can delay the onset of transient cell carcinoma.

He reaped what he sowed. Suddenly Kuppuswamy found himself without the bladder, prostate and several lymph nodes. He had just one kidney; the other kidney was dysfunctional and hence ligated (though this is not connected with his tobacco addiction). Despite missing several body parts, Kuppuswamy managed to lead a decent and respectable life.

Life was not that bad for Kuppuswamy till recently. He had a good academic career. For some time, he was contented being a nuclear research scientist. Then he conducted public awareness programs on the benefits of atomic energy for mankind. Ironically, he spoke a lot about nuclear medicine and radiopharmaceuticals and the use of radioisotopes in diagnosis and therapy, including radio-immunoassays, Cobalt teletherapy and brachytherapy. Little did he know that he may one day need these to cure his ailment.

His wife, Pramila, was a gem of a woman. They had two brilliant children, Arvind and Jagadeesh. Just like their father, they too studied at IIT. Both boys married their classmates and had two children each. While the older boy Arvind and his family lived in Karnahalli, Jagadeesh and his family lived in a small town in Alabama in the United States of America.

After retirement, his father's dream of seeing his son in the field of medicine began to play on Kuppuswamy's mind quite often. Kuppuswamy had saved up quite a bit, though he regretted not having invested his money in real estate. But he still wanted to work. From home preferably and with flexible working hours, as he did not like long commutes to work at an advanced age. He had an excellent command over the English language and loved editing in particular. He wondered if he could do a job that involved a mix of medical terminology and editing.

In the United States, there was a serious shortage of manpower in speedy delivery of patient records. The turnaround time taken by existing manpower was way too high, though it was not clear who was impatient: the doctors, the patients, the hospitals' legal advisors or the insurance companies. Cost was the other challenge. The salaries of secretaries and supporting staff to type and upload patient documents was a big drain on hospital resources.

In the meantime, a few smart Alecs in India saw this as a huge business opportunity. The doctors dictated the patients' medical records and reports, which were then uploaded by the doctor's office or hospital as a voice file by evening (US time). This was when people in India started their work. While the Americans slept, the Indians typed the records. By the time the doctor's office opened the next morning, the typed reports were uploaded and sent to the doctors.

The Indian medical transcriptionists had to be trained to listen carefully and understand different American accents and its idiosyncrasies. They also had to be familiar with medical terminology and the drug index. And this was not a big deal for the Indians.

So Kuppuswamy decided to join the bandwagon. He thought there was a great opportunity in medical transcription. It would bring in decent returns on investment. So he decided to start a medical transcription company.

For starters, he roped in a few senior medical students. These students thought this would be a great learning exercise for them, as they typed the medical reports of patients being diagnosed and treated by American doctors.

Thus began Kuppuswamy's tryst with the medical fraternity. But this didn't last too long as the erratic power availability made it difficult to meet the deadlines. Fearing a bad reputation, Kuppuswamy decided to shut shop gracefully and retain the friendship and association of his former clients. He then relocated to Malgudi where he could spend his retirement days in peace. But God had other plans for him.

Never in his wildest imagination did Kuppuswamy think he would become a victim of bladder cancer revealed first through a couple of episodes of gross hematuria in the years ahead.

Poem - 1

With help from family and friends
With medical treatment and new trends
We'll do our best through smooth and rough
To stay real positive .... hang in tough.
And maybe before our final breath
We may rejoice at cancers death.

– **John Kehoe**, in *Familyfriendpoems.com*

CHAPTER 2
SHOCK AND DISMAY

Not knowing what lies ahead

Yesterday was an extremely hot day in Malgudi. Kuppuswamy was reading his favorite book when he had the accident. It was embarrassing though common in summer. His urostomy bag had opened from the bottom. The adhesive had dissolved in the sweat, exposing a yawning gap that allowed the fluid to sneak through.

The bag had to be disposed safely. His abdomen had to be washed with Dettol water before being cleaned with soap and water. All this had to be done immediately. So Kuppuswamy got down to it. After drying the abdomen, he cleaned up the surrounding area with the tincture of Benzoin.

A raw bit of the stoma protruded from Kuppuswamy's stomach just above the right of the navel. In the absence of a kidney, bladder, prostate and several lymph nodes, urine kept dripping from the stoma regularly, day and night. The amount of urine dripping depended on the fluid intake. Ironically, the patient had no feeling of the dripping urine.

A wafer (some call it a flange) with a hole in the middle (with the same diameter as the protruding stoma) was stuck on the abdomen with a Fevicol-type skin-compatible adhesive (which had now dissolved) and a bag was clipped onto it, with the outlet stopcock firmly closed. The urine collected in the bag. As the bag's weight increased, a gentle tug of the bag warned the wearer that it was time to empty the bag by opening the stopcock.

Normally, Kuppuswamy drained the bag once every three hours after a fluid intake of two to three liters. This process required a decent restroom, as he was more prone to infections than other people.

Since the bag had now torn open, it had to be replaced. After replacing the bag, Kupppuswamy returned to the book by his favorite author Charles Dickens. He was reading a passage from *A Tale of Two Cities*.

It was the best of times, it was the worst of times, it was the age of wisdom, it was the age of foolishness, it was the epoch of belief, it was the epoch of incredulity, it was the season of light, it was the season of darkness, it was the spring of hope, it was the winter of despair, they had everything before them, they had nothing before them, they were all going direct to heaven, they were all going direct the other way.

Kuppuswamy thought to himself that the word 'they' could apply to the group of cancer patients waiting in the outpatient area for the oncologist to arrive. He had felt like this so many times in the past.

Everyone at home had a hurried dinner. It was time for the Skype call with his two grandchildren, aged five and eight.

Krithika, Jagadeesh's daughter, was full of empathy.

"Shall I sing a song for you, *thatha*, my own song?"

"Sure dear."

Krithika sang her song.

"Oh dear *thatha*, don't you cry for me. I will come from Alabama with a bandage on my knee. So what if you can't wear jeans, pants or boxers. We'll see you in Louisiana with the bag that's stuck on you."

"What a beautiful song that is! Did you make it up yourself? I am totally delighted to hear you sing it."

"Yes, *thatha*, I did it all by myself."

"From which original song is this adapted?"

"It is from *Oh Suzanna don't you cry for me*."

Then the younger child, Ashwin, joined the conversation.

"*Thatha*, you must see my dinosaurs. Shall I show them to you?"

"I would surely love to see them."

Unfortunately, it was time for the power cut in Malgudi. As always, the conversation ended abruptly.

In Alabama, the kids screamed that it was not fair that they could no longer see their grandparents on the screen. They could not understand why this happened every time they were on Skype.

Back in Malgudi, everyone was singing Krithika's song together. It was a beautiful adaptation of the original. Kuppuswamy felt very emotional as he shed copious tears involuntarily.

After the abrupt end to the Skype call, Kuppuswamy retired to his bedroom. His mind wandered to the review of his condition: the debris of a broken stent had been left behind in the ileal conduit diversion during the previous stent replacement. Though his mind told him that there was no cause for concern, he was still worried. It could be a nucleus around which a stone could grow. He recalled a news item in that day's newspaper about an eighty-year-old man, Ramaswamy, who had a stent placed in his ureter. One day, Ramaswamy had to leave town for good. In his hurry, he forgot about the scheduled follow-ups for the stent in his body, as the urine flow rates and volume were fine. Eight long years later, he was diagnosed with the growth of a gigantic stone around the long-forgotten double J stent.

Just then Kuppuswamy heard someone in the other room say, "He asked for it, he deserves it." He thought maybe his family was discussing his grandson's award for outstanding innovation. Or perhaps the talk centered on the broken stent debris inside his body. Then he heard a woman's voice, loud and clear, "As you sow, so shall you reap. How many times we implored him to kick the habit? The more we begged, the worse his habit became. What happened now? His smoking that was previously done in the open later became a furtive habit away from anyone's sight after we repeatedly pestered him to quit."

And a male voice responded, "Hasn't he suffered enough? Why do you keep at it all the time? He needs our help and empathy. If his own family keeps harping on what should have been forgotten and forgiven by now, how will he get back to facing people? As it is, he is confined to his room and is embarrassed to come out. To think he was such a social person and a powerful speaker once!"

This conversation set Kuppuswamy thinking. He thought of the events of the past two years. After all, thoughts did invade the cancer conqueror. On his first visit to the hospital, Kuppuswamy met several kinds of cancer patients: those who had been told they could survive for a few more years and those who were terminally ill. The irony of cancer is the patients with a good survival chance die early, all of a sudden, while those with terminal cancer defy all odds and get a new lease of life.

Most often, the difference between succumbing to cancer and conquering it to lead a normal life again is about how soon you recognize the signals. These are often not clearly recognizable. Survival and admitting that you are a cancer patient needing medical care is also about the open communication channels you establish with those near and dear to you. If communication is absent, one quickly gets into the realm of no return.

Do you hide the things that are suddenly growing differently in your body? Do you ignore the lumps or quietly flush the shade of red or pink in your urine or the odd-looking dark brown stools?

When the general physician recommends a consult with the oncologist, what does one generally do? One just brushes it aside. Why does he or she do this? Is it the fear of social stigma? Does he or she not want to scare the family? Or is the prime reason for secrecy the thought of the lakhs of rupees that need to be rustled up in quick time?

But none of the above supersedes the fear of sudden death. This fear pushes one to the brink and forces him or her to visit the oncologist. But by then it is perhaps too late. Then there is no use blaming the stars or suspecting the proficiency of the medical fraternity.

Or is it much ado about nothing? When Kuppuswamy reported a few symptoms, his urine was sent for culture. The result came out 'benign," i.e. sans malignancy. So a false sense of security set in, camouflaging the monster within.

Then the doctors wondered if it could it be bladder cancer. Kuppuswamy set out for a cystoscopy (a view of the insides of the bladder with a camera that goes right in, enabling scraping and sampling of the cells that appear different). He was told that the biopsy result would take three to four days to come.

Meanwhile, there was a battery of pre-operation tests and clearances and then the post-surgery recovery time. Finally, after days of trauma, Kuppuswamy was discharged from the hospital along with a Foley catheter inserted inside him and the urobag.

This was initially a major lifestyle shock to Kuppuswamy. He avoided his grandchildren at home as he felt embarrassed with a catheter and a prominent bag hanging outside. In three days, he went back to the hospital for his biopsy results and catheter removal.

We have all heard of drops of blood in the urine, but Kuppuswamy's experience was mind-blowing. It all began about two years ago. Kuppuswamy was excreting a lot of blood accompanied by very little urine. This happened not once, but twice within a span of about an hour. This was enough to cause Kuppuswamy to faint in fear. But remember, God never tests you with more than what you can bear.

There were three doctors in the family who resided within a ten-minute walking distance from Kuppuswamy's house. If he had any problem, one of them would be by his side in the next fifteen minutes.

It was divine intervention that helped detect Kuppuswamy's illness at a very early stage. The first episode of gross hematuria occurred immediately after the return from Vaitheeswaran Koil (temple) in a hired taxi.

At the Vaitheeswaran temple, the goddess is Balambiga. It is dedicated to Lord Shiva who is worshipped as Vaitheeswaran or

Vaidhyanathaswamy. His consort is also known as Thaiyalnayagi (the goddess with the pot of medicinal oil). Nevertheless, it is Lord Muruga, or Muthukumaraswamy, who is the celebrated deity in the temple. Legend has it that Angarakan, i.e. Mars, had suffered from leprosy and was cured by Vaidhyanathaswamy.

Another story associated with this temple is that Jataayu's wing, which was chopped off by Ravana, landed on this place. The spot where Jataayu was cremated is called the Jataayu Kundam, which is inside the temple.

Back in his apartment after the temple visit, Kuppuswamy was bleeding all the way from the parking lot, through the lift, till his house. Even the cab driver had remarked, "Here a blood, there a blood, everywhere a blood, blood, blood."

Fortunately, Kuppuswamy's wife's sister Narmada stayed on the same street where he stayed. Was it merely fortuitous that the sister's husband was a doctor? Or was it a divine blessing? Narmada's sons too were doctors and all of them practiced in the same town.

Was it God's will that this episode should occur on a Sunday afternoon when all the doctors were at home? Kuppuswamy had the best of circumstances to deal with the frightening situation. Not even a film director could have conceived such a situation for his hero.

His nephew (the doctor) preferred to talk to his *periamma* (Kuppuswamy's wife Pramila) quite some distance away so that Kuppuswamy could not hear what was being discussed. This should have made Kuppuswamy suspect that something was serious. But he was too naïve.

Being a relative of a doctor's family in a small town like Malgudi had its own advantages. The ambulance was at the doorstep even before one could ask if Kuppuswamy needed one. The ultrasound scanning center was also opened, though it was a Sunday. A whole abdomen scan was done so that the urologist could see the report early next morning.

On Monday, the urologist merely said, "Take him home now. I will discuss this with your doctor." Kuppuswamy still did not think anything was severely wrong with him. The first signs of fear entered his mind only when their family doctor called his wife over the phone. The doctor said he wanted to talk to her alone in his clinic.

Pramila went to see the doctor. He told her that Kuppuswamy's condition could not be managed in a small town like Malgudi. They had to move to a bigger place for "some time." Kuppuswamy was told that he could be suffering from carcinoma of the bladder.

And the mind games began. There were questions galore. *Should they move to Talgudi where his brother lived or should they go to Karnahalli where his son resided? Both places were a six-hour drive away from Malgudi. Should Kuppuswamy stay with his brother or his son? How long does 'some time' mean? Does Kuppuswamy need to see just an urologist or would an oncologist also be necessary? Or are they doctors who specialize in both?* Googling the answers only created more doubts than before.

Thankfully, Kuppuswamy didn't question God. He didn't ask Him "why me?" The only thought that plagued his mind was this: wasn't fifteen years of abstinence from tobacco sufficient atonement for his forty-year-old addiction? Apparently not, decided Kuppuswamy. On hindsight, it appeared to him that quitting tobacco only gained him a few more years; it didn't help him escape for life unscathed.

For natural and obvious reasons, it was decided that they would go to his son's place in Karnahalli. Kuppuswamy and his wife feared a civil war if they decided otherwise.

Pramila called her son Jagadeesh in the United States of America.

It was past midnight in Alabama. Jagadeesh was fast asleep when he got a call from India. He normally did not respond to calls so late. But this call was from his mother from Malgudi. He immediately knew something was wrong. So he picked up the call in a flash.

"Hi *amma,* what is the problem? All okay, we hope."

"No Jagadeesh, we faced some extremely tense drama today. *Appa* was urinating just blood. Fortunately, doctor *chithappa* came and examined him immediately."

"Oh my god! Did he take an ultrasound scan?"

"Yes, we have done that. It looks like a malignant mass in the bladder near the outlet. We haven't told *appa* yet."

"I suppose you understand that all of us cannot come to India at the same time at this point. The kids cannot miss school."

"Yes, I understand. Arvind has suggested that we come to his place in Karnahalli and get the cancer specialist he knows to take a look at *appa*. I have booked a cab tomorrow morning. It is a six-hour drive. But we will manage somehow. He seems okay and fit to take the trip."

"One of us will come there after a few days. You get back to us once you get the biopsy reports."

"I'll do that. Take care. Bye for now."

"Bye."

As soon as she hung up the call, the phone rang. She wondered if it was the family doctor. She rushed to answer the phone. The number on the caller ID indicated that the call was from her older son Arvind.

"Arvind here, *amma*. What have you decided?"

"We have booked an Innova cab so that he can lie down through most of the journey if he feels tired. We are leaving early in the morning. We should be there in time for a late lunch. You will have to first register at the hospital. And then get an appointment with your friend, Dr Soman, at the Cancer Institute for the day after tomorrow."

"Okay *amma*, see you tomorrow evening when I get back from work."

Arvind then informed his wife Ramya of his parents' program. The children were excited as Ramya told them the news.

"Thatha is sick and has to be admitted in the hospital. You should not disturb him, okay?"

"But surely he can play cricket with me first and then go to the hospital, right?" asked Pratyush, the younger child.

"Why would anyone want to go see a doctor without playing cricket?" he asked before running out to play.

The children's main concern was where the long Innova car would be parked.

Soon it was time for the trip to the hospital in Karnahalli. To compound matters, the hospital's biopsy results were inconsistent with the results from the first biopsy. The slides were sent to an external lab for a second opinion. This got Kuppuswamy and his wife rushing out of Karnahalli as fast as they could.

Meanwhile, Arvind received an e-mail from Jagadeesh.

Arriving Saturday flight XYZ 345 expected time of arrival is 02:25. I will take a cab and come home. Do not, rpt, do not bother to come to the airport.

Regards.

Arvind immediately replied to Jagadeesh.

Don't come to Karnahalli now. Get to Talgudi first. External lab biopsy report from the slides is incompatible with the hospital report. Appa and amma have no confidence in this doctor or in the hospital. They are moving to chithi's place in Talgudi for further action. Chithappa will identify the oncologist and the urologist.

Love to you and the kids. Take care and bye.

Jagadeesh to Arvind:

Rerouting doesn't seem feasible. Coming to Karnahalli. I shall escort appa and amma to Talgudi. I will talk to the oncologist myself. See you in person.

Arvind to Jagadeesh:

Okay. What happened on Halloween? Hugs and kisses to the kids. See you later.

CHAPTER 3
RAY OF HOPE

Plan of action clear

Was Kuppuswamy losing valuable time while planning to proceed to Talgudi? Enquiries revealed that a major corporate hospital in Talgudi had a two-in-one specialist. He was both a urologist and an oncologist. This was exactly what was needed. It appeared as a silver lining in the dark clouds looming ahead. But was Kuppuswamy aware of the long journey in the dark tunnel before he saw some light? No one knew what was in store. No one knew that there would be minor accidents with his ancillary addendum, no one knew he would have to get back home within three hours every time he went out.

Meanwhile, tension mounted every second for Kuppuswamy and his family. They were worried if the delay in proceeding to Talgudi would cost Kuppuswamy a lot, with an advance in cancer and its consequences. They were on tenterhooks all the time. They wondered if they had lost faith in the Karnahalli hospital a little too soon.

But what else could Kuppuswamy have done? Two reports with two different interpretations on the same specimen was bound to make anyone lose faith. Either the histopathologist or the onco-surgeon had gone wrong. But it didn't matter who was wrong. The underlying faith had been lost. Kuppuswamy felt he was justified in not continuing his treatment at that hospital. Faith and trust in the surgeon are of paramount importance, particularly more so when dealing with a dreaded disease.

At Arvind's house, the doorbell rang very early in the morning. It was just 4 a.m., but the entire household, including four-year-old Pratyush, was awake. Pratyush's *chithappa* from Alabama had landed. He would be at the doorstep any time now.

Thatha wasn't comfortable playing cricket with him and his brother these days. *Paati* didn't know how to bowl straight at the bat; she always went cockeyed and hit the stumps instead! *Chithappa* played baseball in America and he would know exactly how to hit the bat with the ball, thought little Pratyush.

And in walked Jagadeesh. In the midst of the gloom, a ray of optimism emerged with his arrival. But he was alone. The children couldn't believe their eyes.

"*Chithappa*, that driver uncle took away *paati's* white Innova car as soon as she went into the bathroom. You have to fight with him and get it back." These were the words that Pratyush welcomed Jagadeesh with.

"Just hold on, Pratyush. Let me WhatsApp *chithi* and the kids back home first. And then we'll talk about the car thief. Did you drink your milk yet?"

"No *chithappa*, not milk. Boost is the secret of my energy and Complan gives me extra energy. You have never seen these Indian TV ads, so you don't know these famous proverbs."

While uncle and nephew were discussing the advertisements on Indian TV, Kuppuswamy wrote an e-mail to Govindaswamy. Govindaswamy was the husband of Renuka, who was Pramila's sister. Soon Renuka and Govindaswamy would become Kuppuswamy's prime caregivers in Talgudi, apart from Pramila herself.

From Kuppuswamy to Govindaswamy:

Jagadeesh arrived this morning from Alabama. He will accompany us to Talgudi tomorrow. As always, we will leave after an early breakfast. We shall also eat our lunch en route so as to give me some leg stretching exercises.

Appointment with the oncologist at the extension clinic opposite your house is in the evening. Sorry for the inconvenience being caused.

From Renuka to Kuppuswamy:

Most welcome, athimber. Don't worry about anything. Everything will be taken care of. See you soon.

Soon Kuppuswamy and his family reached Talgudi. Along with Govindaswamy, they visited the uro-oncologist.

The uro-oncologist said he could not proceed on the basis of the existing contradictory reports. How could the surgeon trust the reports when Kuppuswamy himself thought they were just worthless sheets of paper?

Kuppuswamy had to be admitted in the hospital for a repeat cystoscopy (TURBT in more precise medical parlance) for a biopsy report from pathology. But his insides were still raw from the first intervention. Hence, they would have to wait for six weeks before his insides could be probed again. This only meant more time lost. Would this have any detrimental consequences? Fear began to creep into everyone's minds.

The surgeon firmly said, "Well Mr Kuppuswamy, I am a surgeon trained in the United Kingdom. I follow the British protocol. Things here will be different from what your doctor at Karnahalli may have followed. The details are on this sheet. You can go through them at leisure. I have to see for myself what the insides look like. We will wait for six weeks before repeating the cystoscopy. And then we can decide what to do. In the meantime, you can choose a date in the sixth or seventh week from now for admission. How do you plan to fund your treatment?"

"Most likely from my own savings for immediate liabilities. And then my pension accruals going forward," said Kuppuswamy.

"We will look after it. No issues, doctor," said Jagadeesh.

The family hoped for the best, but also prepared for the worst. The worst case scenario was carcinoma in situ with invasion into the muscle. Anything else could be attempted to be arrested with chemotherapy and radiation therapy. They were told that the side effects and the pain could be worse than the actual disease. What were the chances of survival? There was no definite answer. They were cautioned that it was not uncommon for patients to develop suicidal tendencies by the time they reached the fourth or fifth dose of radiation.

If after a year of chemotherapy and radiation, the cancer was not entirely eliminated, the affected organ and its surroundings had to be removed. Also the organs where the cancer had metastasized (migrated) to had to be exposed to radiation to prevent further spread. The family had to be prepared for a never-ending cycle. The other option was to remove the organ and its surroundings to lead a fairly decent and dignified life without too much of a change in the quality of life, in particular the day-to-day activities. The cards were on the table and Kuppuswamy and his family had to decide.

Six weeks later, Kuppuswamy was admitted into the large hospital with a strong sense of déjà vu.

The nurse came in and asked, "No blood pressure, sir?" Kuppuswamy said, "Yes hypertension, but under control with medication. Except when the white coat syndrome takes over. And no diabetes." The nurse then asked, "No dentures?" He said, "You are right. No dentures and no contact lenses too." The nurse then departed with a smile. Before leaving she said, "Don't worry, sir. Neckties by physicians are banned in this hospital. That source of infection is thus effectively out of bounds."

The same anesthesiology pre-operation routine with the same queries and tests began. The only difference was all the patients in this hospital were cancer patients.

Kuppuswamy's roommate was a sixteen-year-old girl. Across the corridor, on the other side, was a baby. The baby was less than two weeks old and had not yet been named.

The atmosphere in the hospital spelt irrational fear with an anticipation of impending gloom. Kuppuswamy felt like the nobleman awaiting the call of the guillotine during the French Revolution, as described in the novel by Charles Dickens. Screams of pain emanated from the other half of the room. His roommate was just back from a chemo session. She was throwing up a green fluid. It was the anti-vomit medicine that caused whatever was eaten to be expelled. What an irony, thought Kuppuswamy.

Kuppuswamy's first brush with cancer treatment, albeit at a distance, was awful and terrifying. That night he dreamt of a huge drilling machine with a small brachytherapy unit: radioactive pellets at the tip boring into his abdomen and playing with his intestines like they were soiled noodles that had to be discarded and burnt to cinders.

Kuppuswamy was back from the operation theater (OT) with tubes all over. Two from above till the wrist for feeding and for administering pain medication, a catheter down by his right side connected to the urobag and another tube down the left with a container to trap blood and other discharges from the surgical site. He was also on an oxygen mask for some time. It was a terrible sight for his family but not too bad for the patient himself, except that it restricted free movement.

This time, the four days in hospital went by really fast. The biopsy confirmed a bladder carcinoma in situ. The family had made its decision: off with the bladder. Kuppuswamy was given a six-week break for the cystoscopic intervention to heal. His bladder had to be taken out within ninety days. Arvind was away on a long work-related trip abroad. He would be back in seventy-five days.

The family decided to stay in Talgudi till the first quarterly review after the surgery. So the hunt for a house for six months began.

The surgeon detailed the procedure. It was very illuminating. He was contemplating a radical cystectomy, which involved the removal of the entire bladder and possibly the nearby tissues and organs. For men, the prostate and urethra also had to be removed, apart from the lymph nodes in the pelvis.

In robot-assisted cystectomy, which is what the family had opted for, the surgeon makes a few small incisions instead of one large incision in an open surgery. Using a telescope-like equipment, the bladder and the surrounding tissues are removed.

Once the bladder is removed, a new plumbing system to push the urine out of the body is created. This is known as an ileal conduit diversion. A section of the small intestine or colon is utilized to divert urine to a stoma, which is made to protrude just outside the body. This is in most cases, not always, just above the right side of the navel. This essentially meant that Kuppuswamy had to wear a bag attached to the stoma to collect and drain urine at regular intervals.

The stoma is made from a part of the small intestine called the ileum. The ureter attached to a small piece of the ileum is pulled through the skin of the abdomen; hence the name ileal conduit diversion.

The stoma is very delicate, pinkish-red and moist. One can expect mucus, spots of blood and even a small amount of bleeding from the stoma, said the doctor. This made Kuppuswamy jittery till he was convinced that such bleeding would be in minute quantities.

Kuppuswamy feared his abdomen brushing against things such as the wash basin, dining table or kitchen platform and causing pain. The doctor reassured him that since the stoma had no nerve endings, he would not feel anything.

Kuppuswamy had a real choice, not just a Hobson's choice, between conventional open surgery and robotic surgery. But decisive parameters such as lesser blood loss, better pain management, shorter hospital stay and faster recovery helped Kuppuswamy and his family opt for robot-assisted radical cystectomy. The only major issues were that the surgery would take a wee bit longer and it would cost almost twenty per cent more. Kuppuswamy was told that the surgery would be over in about four or five hours, but it lasted nine hours. But then that is a different story.

CHAPTER 4

PRELUDE TO A LONG DAY

All set for the major surgery

The big nine-hour surgery, involving the use of a robot to remove the bladder, prostate and lymph nodes and ligate the ureter from a dysfunctional kidney, was still a few weeks away. But no one knew, at that point of time, that one of Kuppuswamy's kidneys was already non-functional. As they say, it never rains, it only pours.

The forced stay in Talgudi meant looking for a house near Kuppuswamy's sister-in-law's house. This need was accentuated by the fact that while on BCG (Bacillus Calmette-Guerine), great care had to be taken so that the others in the house were not exposed to the live bacteria.. Kuppuswamy also needed a dedicated restroom for use every four hours. Kuppuswamy's clothes and bed linen had to be washed separately. It was not going to be easy. After all, the family was dealing with live BCG, the same vaccine used for tuberculosis. Though he could have stayed with his sister-in-law or his brother, Kuppuswamy didn't want to make it difficult for either of them.

But as the period of stay would not even be a year, it was not easy to find a two-bedroom house. No one was willing to let out their house for such a short term. In spite of all this they did manage to find a suitable house soon.

Next, the family had to find a full-time cook-cum-maid-cum-attendant. They also had to rent or borrow furniture. This is where Kuppuswamy's brothers and his wife's sisters contributed. All of them parted with their surplus, right from a gas stove, cylinder, cooking utensils and containers for groceries to a refrigerator, essential furniture such as dining table and chairs, cots and mattresses and bed linen. Even buckets and mugs were given.

An air-conditioner was hired as a sub-20-degree Celsius temperature was required to keep infections at bay.

A television with cable connection too was given though Kuppuswamy barely spent even ten minutes a day watching TV after his surgery. Someone even lent a laptop with a dongle. But soon Kuppuswamy realized how painful being online was as everybody wanted to talk directly to him and his wife. He was always too tired to enjoy a Skype session, even with his grandchildren.

The contribution of his children and their spouses, physically, mentally and financially, was spontaneous and immense. His children took care of the hospital expense of four lakh rupees without batting an eyelid. His daughters-in-law displayed tremendous family values. His older grandson, Ankit, the brother of Pratyush, who was in class eleven, also played a big role in his recovery.

Pramila's sister and her husband provided ample support to Pramila whose mind was always in a turmoil.

Tension, uncertainty and fear were at their peak. There were several possible complications from the surgery. The surgeon did not rule out life-threatening risks. Kuppuswamy had a history of transient ischemic attack (similar to a stroke) in the recent past and Milliary Koch's disease (a strain of tuberculosis) several years ago. And of course, people over seventy faced additional age-related issues. Though Kuppuswamy's hypertension (elevated blood pressure) was under control generally, it wavered in the last few days before surgery. He did not have diabetes yet, but his blood-glucose levels skyrocketed just before any surgery. And only time would tell what surprises lay in store when the surgeon cut open Kuppuswamy's abdomen to redesign God's plumbing.

The D-day would arrive in ten days. The date was finalized immediately on Arvind's return from his foreign assignment. The admission procedures were completed. The family was in for a long haul. It was a bitter pill but it had to be swallowed. Little did the family know that whatever Kuppuswamy smelt and tasted would be unbearable post-surgery, thanks to dysgeusia. Little did Kuppuswamy know that whatever his wife fed him with would be promptly expelled.

Poem - 2

Cancer invades uninvited and unwanted,
An intruder in my body,
Waiting to claim me,
A complete stranger, though
It weaves a web of intricate pain.

I enter the battlefield in fury,
The scans and labs a learning step,
To score a goal against the monster,
Finding the essence of life,
In my inner sanctum,
I cease to exist, I now live.

– **Geetha Paniker**, in *When I fell in Love with Life*

CHAPTER 5
D-DAY

Robotic radical cystectomy

Kuppuswamy took out his daily tear-off calendar. He wrote the number '10' under the current date, '9' under the next date and so on. He wrote '0' under the date of surgery. The countdown had begun.

The new helper, Kamala, had settled down in the household routine. She had to buy milk in the morning, vegetables later in the day, get drinking water from the shop across and do odd jobs in the kitchen. She was also entrusted with the job of hanging the washed clothes on the clothesline to dry, folding dried clothes and stacking them in the cupboard in the evening. She was slowly getting trained to run the kitchen independently. She would be required to do so during the two weeks of hospitalization. She was well-prepared for the days ahead.

It was time for the pre-op anesthesiology evaluation. All of a sudden, the anesthetist was a little reticent to approve a major surgery. He wanted a neurologist's report, a cardiologist's assessment and a clearance from the nephrologist. So the march to the neurologist began. The neurologist wanted a carotid Doppler. Kuppuswamy then went to the cardiologist who in turn wanted an ECG done right away. Looking at the ECG, the cardiologist suggested that an echo be taken. The nephrologist, after ensuring that there was no problem with the output volume, incontinence or a bloated abdomen, just added some medication to be taken till surgery. In three days, Kuppuswamy was cleared for surgery. The daily calendar on which Kuppuswamy had written a few days ago read '6' in red. The roster of who would be with

Kuppuswamy in the hospital at what time was drawn. And there was no shortage of volunteers.

Shakespeare in the prologue to Henry V said,

.......pardon, gentles all,

The flat unraised spirits that have dared

On this unworthy scaffold to bring forth

So great an object.

Kuppuswamy went to sleep. He had a long undisturbed sleep, now that the path to the surgery and liberation from the dreaded cancer had been cleared. He did not know whom to thank and how. He was all set to go to war against the silent killer devil.

Kuppuswamy was put on a 'nil by mouth' regimen. A well-wisher from abroad called Kuppuswamy and reminded him of Henry V's advice to his soldiers on the eve of the Battle of Agincourt.

When the blast of war blows in our ears,
Then imitate the action of the tiger;
Stiffen the sinews, summon up the blood,
Disguise fair nature with hard-favored rage;
Then lend the eye a terrible aspect;
Let pry through the portage of the head like the brass cannon.

And this cheered him up.

The all-too-familiar déjà vu-inducing routine began. A post-graduate student doctor took notes on Kuppuswamy's medical history. Close to midnight, Kuppuswamy was put under the watch of a night duty registrar—a surgeon who was sharpening his skills under the onco-surgeon. Strangely, he seemed in awe of the patient. He refused to answer any question, be it related to urology or to oncology. There was just one answer from him, "Ask sir when you meet him in the OT in the morning."

Kuppuswamy never got to see his surgeon till thirty hours later. By then, he didn't care anymore. His organs had been rubbished already for all practical purposes.

An internal medicine resident physician mumbled to himself as he examined Kuppuswamy, "Pupils are symmetric, round and responsive to light and accommodation, airways canals are clear, the oropharynx is pink, past history of SMR (sub-mucous resection of turbinates) and calvilac for sinusitis and a deviated septum, neck is supple, no JVD, not clear why the anesthetist wanted a carotid Doppler, cardiovascular system regular, S1, S2 present. ECG with no abnormalities other than age-related ones detected, lungs are clear as per chest x-ray, no scarring of ancient Koch's disease, now treated, abdomen is soft, non-tender, the wrinkle-free area to the right of the navel marked for stoma exit, no hepatosplenomegaly, no penile sores or rashes, past history of bilateral hernia repair, no DVT, nail beds are pink, no pedal edema."

This reminded Kuppuswamy of Operation Overlord on June 6, 1944 when combined troops from the UK, the USA and Canada landed at five places on the beaches of Normandy. Dwight Eisenhower in his Order of the Day had remarked:

You are about to embark upon the Great Crusade, toward which we have striven these many months. The eyes of the world are upon you. The hopes and prayers of liberty-loving people everywhere march with you... Your task will not be an easy one. Your enemy is well trained, well equipped and battle-hardened. He will fight savagely.

Kuppuswamy also thought of August 1945, when Hiroshima and Nagasaki were bombed, on the heels of Pearl Harbor.

In came the dreaded stretcher. Kuppuswamy got on to it and bid au revoir to those around him. In the corridors of the OT, Kuppuswamy experienced the worst wait of his life. People in uniform were bustling here and there. No one even gave him a second glance. Someone just said, "He is not Dr Varma's patient." Patients in stretchers were moved out, some were pushed in. A nurse screamed in heavy Malayali accent, "Doctor has arrived *dee*."

Kuppuswamy was wheeled in to the OT and dumped on the operation table. The anesthetist made small talk with him. Then she got into a conversation with someone on her mobile phone with a distinct British accent.

Kuppuswamy recited a few lines from Macaulay's *Lays of Ancient Rome* before he lost consciousness.

Lars Porsena of Clusium
By the Nine Gods he swore
That the great house of Tarquin
Should suffer wrong no more.
By the Nine Gods, he swore it,
And named a trysting day,
And bade his messengers ride forth,
East and west and south and north,
To summon his array.

He dreamt of all that had happened so far. Then he experienced an extrasensory perception of what was going on. There was a fleeting glimpse of Tennyson in his mind.

Home they brought her warrior dead:
She nor swooned, nor uttered cry:
All her maidens, watching, said,
She must weep or she will die.
Then they praised him, soft and low,
Called him worthy to be loved,
Truest friend and noblest foe;
Yet she neither spoke nor moved.

This lasted only for a brief while. He had no cognizance of when he was pushed out into the post-surgery recovery room nine hours later.

Pramila had been told that the surgery would take about four or five hours and that she could go home for a bath and breakfast and get back after lunch.

In an unconscious state, Kuppuswamy dreamt or perhaps hallucinated that he was on a closed circuit TV with a surgeon explaining what was being done to him to a group of students from various disciplines. The doctor was stressing the need to apply a plumber's intuition when dealing with surprises during the course of a radical cystectomy with ileal conduit diversion. The students were extremely happy to have this opportunity as urology wasn't part of their rotational house surgeoncy in undergraduate medical colleges. Oncology students were curious to see how the environment changed as they scraped and resected the bladder and prostate and the surrounding lymph nodes.

In the past, every resident doctor was given a TNM Handbook to identify the stage of cancer in the patient. (TNM stands for tumor, node and metastasis.) This book was used to classify the malignant tumors. With sixty-five types of cancers, it was not possible for doctors to remember the various permutations and combinations. Having the handbook helped young doctors. But now, there was no need to carry the handbook as smartphones had replaced it. The TNM App developed by a Mumbai cancer research center and hospital was on all the doctors' phones. But no app could match the education that watching a live surgery provided.

Kuppuswamy was under general anesthesia. He was on his back with his hips and knees flexed and thighs apart, much like it happens during childbirth. In a dreamy state of hallucination Kuppuswamy heard some commentary.

"It should be remembered that the procedure today is robotic. Also bear in mind that the system cannot be pre-programmed. Nor can it make decisions independently. Every surgical intervention requires the surgeon to feed the inputs then and there. Small incisions are sufficient to introduce miniaturized wristed instruments and a high-definition 3D camera.

First of all, we begin with a standard port placement. Then the bladder needs to be mobilized all around, after clipping and cutting the vascular pedicles.

Note the ureter being divided above the vesico-ureteric junction. Next goes the endopelvic fascia and finally the puboprostatic ligament.

The dorsal vein complex is now ready to be ligated and once that is done we shall mobilize the prostate all around and divide the ureter…

Good, great going, so far.

As always, we then insert the rectal catheter and perform the methylene blue test. Doctors in the audience, watch out for leaks…

Hurrah! There is no leak. They are now deploying the specimen in a bag. We have been progressing very nicely. Let us take a break now."

As the surgery team munched on the much-needed sandwiches, the medical group monitoring Kuppuswamy let out a cry, "Pressure is wavering. Glucose is on an upward march. Call endocrinology, call diabetology. Pressure is now restored. It is stable and under control. The heart has a regular rhythm. Pulse rate normal. Glucose levels on a watchful wait. The patient is feeling ultra-cold, trembling, shivering."

Kuppuswamy wondered whether it was possible to feel low temperatures under general anesthesia. Someone said, "There is nothing we can do about it, the low temperature is needed for effective infection control."

Why not throw in a blanket, Kuppuswamy wondered.

Outside the OT, Pramila looked at the clock every five minutes wondering when the ordeal would be over.

Back at the operating table…

"We now begin by mobilizing the ureters bilaterally and start dissecting the pelvic lymph nodes on both sides. Tough job, unable to retrieve specimen. So what? Watch what they are doing. It is simple, right? Just extend one of the ports.

Now we begin to prepare the ileal conduit. Up, up and up the right ureter, almost at the kidney itself. All dry. It is obvious now that one kidney that was believed to be underperforming is, in fact, dysfunctional, dysplastic. Probably the effect of the Milliary Koch's of long ago. No time to brood over that. What do we do with this useless kidney?"

It was long past the five-hour estimate. Pramila was covered in sweat.

The surgeon too realized that the surgery was taking longer than expected. It was time for him to walk out and brief the patient's wife.

A nurse came out yelling at the top of her voice, "Patient Kuppuswamy. Is patient Kuppuswamy here? Where is the patient Kuppuswamy?" Someone said that the patient was on the operating table. The nurse then howled, "It means the patient's attendant." She was quite unlike the friendly 'sister' that one often believed nurses to be.

The surgeon himself came out and recognized Pramila. He told her, "All is okay. One of his kidneys is not working, that is all. It is just taking a little longer than we thought. There is absolutely nothing to get agitated over."

A small boy nearby overheard the surgeon. He was another patient's grandchild. He exclaimed, "No kidney? Then he don't need a restroom ever." To which another child retorted, "Come on, he will have a new bag that collects the choo-choo from his stomach. I saw it when Sunil's grandfather came to Karnahalli."

The surgeon and Pramila chuckled hearing this conversation. Children indeed relieved the tension of those waiting outside the OT.

The surgeon got back into the OT.

A friendly-looking woman approached Pramila. "I am Kavitha, stoma care counselor. When the eyes dim with age, spectacles come to the fore. When one gets hard of hearing, the hearing aids take control. When the teeth refuse to mash, dentures come to the rescue. When the legs are disfigured, Jaipuri legs lend support. When none of the above cause any embarrassments, why should ostomy bags, used when the excretory system malfunctions, make you feel like the odd one out? It will be all right."

Cut back to the operating table.

"Doctors in the audience, please recall. Before we took a break, the right ureter was found to be dysplastic with no urine output. The ureter from this kidney is being ligated. Now you can see the spatulation of the left ureter, which will then be anastomosed to the ileal conduit. Finally, the conduit is being brought out as an ostomy in the right lower abdomen."

The junior surgeons stepped in now as the principal surgeon heaved a sigh of relief. Only the incision had to be closed now in layers.

Still in his state of hallucination, Kuppuswamy wondered why he had a dysplastic kidney. He knew that one of his kidneys had multiple cysts and was functioning below par, but he was surprised that he had been living on a solitary kidney for God knows how long. This was indeed a major surprise.

Why did his glucose levels always shoot up in the OT, whether it was a simple SMR, hernia repair or an intervention for prostatitis? More recently, it recurred during both the TURBT (transurethral resection of bladder tumors) procedures. Was it renal glycosuria without diabetes? The diabetologist would not be perturbed unless the blood sugar levels crossed 200. Just like it happened in gestational diabetes, Kuppuswamy's sugar levels normalized once he was out of the post-operative recovery room—on all occasions. Whether this happened through medical intervention or resolved on its own, Kuppuswamy was not too sure. The doctors concluded that this was stress-induced diabetes.

CHAPTER 6
IS THE WORST OVER?

The day after the surgery

Was the worst over? This was the question in every family member's mind. For the team of doctors who were equally exhausted and delighted after a tricky job done well, this perhaps was just another usual day in the office. But for the patient and those near and dear to him, it was a momentous occasion.

Kuppuswamy was terribly angry when he opened his eyes. He saw four beds to the left and five beds across him: all were occupied. He had paid for a twin-sharing room—there ought to have been only one other patient in the room.

The monitors from the surrounding beds were squeaking away. He growled at the nurses by his bedside. It took them quite a while to convince him that he was still in the post-operative recovery room.

"So, when do I go to my own room?" he asked. Hearing the commotion, the anesthesiologist advanced towards him. She was perhaps in her late twenties or early thirties.

"Hello sir, how are we now?" she asked. The word 'we' usually broke all barriers and established closeness.

"I was just trying to find out when I would get to my own room so that my wife's worries are put to rest. My daughter-in-law too must be terribly concerned out there. Also doctor, from time to time I feel as if someone is pressing the calf muscles on my left leg. With a periodic rhythm. It is a little too hard for comfort."

The doctor smiled and said it was the blood pressure monitor and that he would be shifted to his room the moment he could raise his legs.

"Aahaa," said Kuppuswamy, "that should be easy."

But his lower extremities felt like they were bound to a rock. Anyway, that was the condition for his release. Till he could lift his legs, he had to wait. The doctor's assurance eased his mind somewhat. His wife and his daughter-in-law were permitted to see him separately for a couple of minutes each.

And all of a sudden, without any warning, involuntarily, his legs crossed. He stared down in disbelief. "I can move my legs, I can flex them at the knees and I can twiddle my toes." But no one was by his bedside. It was dinner time and half the nurses and the duty doctors were on a break, while the registrars and consultants had left.

Kuppuswamy remembered that he had been on a 'nil by mouth' regimen for twenty-six hours now. His lips were absolutely dry and nearly cracked. Even swallowing saliva seemed a Guinness record breaking event. Thankfully, a nurse passing by asked him if he would like to dampen his lips. He got exactly three drops of water to his lips!

After a dozen phone calls by the nurse, the stretcher was made available. Slowly, Kuppuswamy was moved to the safety of his room. Having experienced two TURBTs in the last three months, he was not taken aback by the Foley catheter on one side and the discharge tube containing blood and other junky mucous fluids from the surgery site on the other. There were IV tubes, one for the medication and another for pushing saline (glucose) fluids into his body. This time there was no oxygen mask, as enough time had elapsed after surgery. The anesthesia, which was generally quantized for doses of forty-five minutes, had fully worn off. And pain began to set in.

The nurses' station had a set of instructions to be followed. Kuppuswamy was given opioid (morphine + fentanyl), one of the most efficient analgesics. First, an intravenous dose was given, followed by an intra-muscular dose after midnight. One mode of administration acted immediately but lasted for a shorter period, while the other took some time to start action but was effective for a longer time period.

The dietician who arrived shortly thereafter said that liquids could be given to Kuppuswamy. Soon tender coconut water was brought to the room. But as they say, there is many a slip between the cup and the lip. A nurse came rushing in and said that Kuppuswamy's potassium levels were elevated and hence coconut water and bananas had to be avoided. So Kuppuswamy had to contend with just a few sips of water.

Kuppuswamy's input-output volumes were monitored. His blood sugar was continuously checked. Blood pressure was textbook numbers and he had no fever. But Kuppuswamy noticed something odd. The catheter tube didn't seem to commence from the penile opening. He strained to trace its origin. It appeared to come out of the abdomen. So Kuppuswamy wondered if urination had to be from the abdomen's right upper quadrant henceforth. It was too monstrous a situation to envisage. Under the weight of this thought, coupled with the action of the sedative, Kuppuswamy dozed off.

When he woke up the next morning, Kuppuswamy tried to have some coffee. It tasted like dishwater and smelt like the contents of the municipal garbage bin. With a loud frightening noise, he threw up what he had consumed back into the cup. Except that it did not look like coffee on the return journey. It was an absolutely green stuff that reminded him of the movie *Exorcist*.

Pramila raced to the nursing station and informed the nurses about Kuppuswamy's situation. But the nurses were least perturbed. On persistent questioning, they insisted that it was because of the pain medication and the medicine given to restrict the vomiting. The opioid medicine caused nausea and induced vomiting in many patients.

While this explanation put to rest Kuppuswamy's worry temporarily, the constant rejection of food in the form of green vomit and the discomfort it was causing was difficult for him to tolerate. The intravenous drips were the main source of sustenance for two more days. Since the sugar levels had abated, the diabetologist's reference was cancelled. All vitals were within normal limits and the blood tests results returned numbers as expected. Because of the solitary kidney, the elevated creatinine and urea levels were causes of great concern and needed constant monitoring. His sodium levels were fine. Potassium was now hovering on the borderline, while calcium and phosphorous were well within the normal range.

Only when the surgeon visited Kuppuswamy was he informed of his dysplastic kidney. The surgeon told him this had surprised them during the surgery, necessitating greater care as they moved forward. The specimen, consisting of the bladder, prostate and lymph nodes, had been sent for biopsy and the results would be known in about three days' time. The surgeon also emphasized that his recovery from the trauma of the surgery would be faster if Kuppuswamy got back on his feet soon. The medicos had done their bit and the ball was now in the patient's court. Then the uro-oncosurgeon left after wishing Kuppuswamy a good day.

The physiotherapist was scheduled to visit Kuppuswamy in the evening to fix appointments for the next few days. The medical and radiation oncologists would come in for an informal counseling session in the afternoon.

Soon it was time for the physiotherapist's arrival. Kuppuswamy was told the physiotherapist was on his way. But three hours passed and there was no sign of him. He was told the physio was on the way. On the way from where, Kuppuswamy wondered. A couple of floors below!

When the physiotherapist arrived finally, Kuppuswamy was eager to get going. He had to get on his feet to speed up his recovery. "But not so fast, sir," the physiotherapist said. "Today we will do some leg exercises. Bending at the knees ten times and twiddling the toes and the fingers of both hands. Do this almost all the time till you are exhausted, but don't overdo it." He also gave Kuppuswamy a toy into which he had to breathe. This would keep pulmonary embolism and pneumonia complications at bay, said the physio.

CHAPTER 7

TEN DAYS AFTER SURGERY

The battle

Day two began nice and bright. The ban on food that contained potassium was lifted as serum K had crept back to normal limits in the latest blood work. Of course, as expected, the creatinine and urea levels were elevated. There was nothing remarkable in the results for calcium and phosphorus. Urine collections were normal in color and volume. Kuppuswamy's irrigation was stepped up. The very crucial bowel movement was awaited. But this could not happen unless something substantial went in.

As they waited for the arrival of the physiotherapist, Pramila referred to a surgeon's talk at a meeting held recently. She had seen a video posted on Facebook while she was waiting in the lobby just outside the OT the other day. The talk was for a captive audience of surgeons only.

The surgeon had advised doctors on maintaining and managing their presence and prestige on social media platforms. The meeting had also discussed issues concerning patient privacy and confidentiality and the need to guard the personal details of the doctor's family.

One doctor had lamented that when a patient was asked for feedback, he or she mechanically said the medical care was okay; they complained vociferously about the air-conditioning in the room not working or the breakfast arriving twenty minutes late. They also complained that the housekeeping staff were arrogant and ill-behaved, the surgeon refused to take calls from the inpatient, the nursing station staff were scared to call the surgeons repeatedly or the physiotherapist had to be called ten times before he actually came. While these were genuine concerns, they were not relevant to the assessment of medical procedures and there was nothing that the doctors could do. They were all mainly management issues.

The Kuppuswamys then wandered to other topics. They wondered why Kuppuswamy was classified as Dr Vivek's patient in the hospital if Dr Vivek could not or did not take care of all the patient's needs. Didn't all the co-ordination with the other doctors, paramedics and dietetics come under Dr Vivek's jurisdiction? Why did he then palm his work off to others as though he wasn't responsible for it? Again, wasn't Dr Vivek responsible for whatever was written on the discharge summary, even if a junior colleague had signed it, Kuppuswamy wondered. Sometimes a lot of gibberish was written on the discharge summary. If the patient questioned it, he was met with disbelieving eyes. The doctors may argue that there were so many forms and proformas to be filled up that it wasn't possible for them to read every word of every discharge summary.

Finally, the physiotherapist arrived. He made Kuppuswamy do some knee bending exercises and twiddle the toes and the fingers. Kuppuswamy's fingers were still numb. They were tingling at the extremities, more on the left hand than the right. There were many questions on everyone's minds. Was it just because of the cold weather or was a neurology consult required? Or would it resolve on its own?

Kuppuswamy was now ready to get vertical. He had been lying on his back for too long, leading to pain in the lower back and the flanks. Pramila was tensed, as though she was watching the climax scene of an action movie. Lying down on his back, Kuppuswamy turned to his left first. He then bent at the knees and slowly got up. He sat for a while before venturing to put his feet on the ground.

It was as though he had stepped on quicksand and the ground below was sinking. He felt as though the room was spinning around him. Pain gripped his calf muscles and his thighs, for a little more than a moment. Kuppuswamy managed to survive the 'quake.' The physiotherapist looked unperturbed. He probably knew exactly what to expect.

Now Kuppuswamy's two 'handbags' had to be carried. One bag collected the drainage and the other was the urobag collection via the catheter from the stoma. Much like a convoy accompanying the District Collector, Pramila held Kuppuswamy, the nurse held the urobag and another nurse carried the discharge container. Someone from housekeeping held the door open. And in an imperial fashion, much like Akbar entering the *durbar* hall, Kuppuswamy walked along the corridor outside his room. He took just a few steps but he couldn't turn to the left. Holding onto the wall, Kuppuswamy slowly scrambled back to his room. He remained sitting for a while. He felt short of breath. He was laid on the bed and given an oxygen mask for a few minutes. Then the physiotherapist said, "See you in the evening."

Again in the evening? Kuppuswamy groaned at the very thought of it. It seemed to him as though hell was empty and all the devils were here in his room, much like how Caliban felt in Shakespeare's *Tempest*.

But the love and affection of Shyamala, the wife of Kuppuswamy's cousin Vijay did the trick. She did a gentle examination of Kuppuswamy's condition. After an in-depth study, she prescribed a homeopathic medication that would give him the ability to withstand all the rigors and trauma of multiple organ resections. And it worked like magic, for soon Kuppuswamy was on his feet and walking the length of the hospital corridor.

Kuppuswamy's wife soon set up a routine. It was now possible for her to leave Kuppuswamy alone for a few minutes for a quick coffee break. Every day, she went home in the morning for a bath and breakfast. She would then return to the hospital with packed lunch.

Whenever Pramila was away, the relatives took turns to be Kuppuswamy's attendant. This also diverted Kuppuswamy's attention as he had a new person to talk to. He or she would bring along the newspaper and soon discussions followed on the headlines of the day. There was also Wi-Fi available for inpatients at the hospital.

This enabled Kuppuswamy to e-mail his children and let them know his status. He also communicated with his brother and sister in the US, his brother in Australia, apart from uncles, aunts and cousins all over the country.

Bilious vomiting (the frightening green fluid) continued. But Kuppuswamy decided to grin and bear the pain and not ask for opioid or any other pain medication. He hoped the pain would resolve on its own.

And it did. On day three, Kuppuswamy woke up without any pain. He was moved to a soft liquid diet. His liquid intake limits were removed. In fact, he was prescribed an increased liquid diet—minimum two liters of fluid a day.

All his vital signs were fine. The urine flow was promising; it was pale though not pale enough. It had a prominent yellow color. There was no signs of a clot or hematuria. The drainage seemed to have stopped and the tube and the attached drainage bag was likely to be removed. Kuppuswamy was eager to be up and sitting.

The oncologists (both medical and radiation) visited Kuppuswamy again. Though the biopsy results had still not come in, the doctors prepared themselves for possible residue and metastasis and the need for maintenance doses. They also hinted to Kuppuswamy that he may have to stay in town for at least another six to eight weeks till the medical oncologists were satisfied.

The oncologists then plunged into a discussion on the differences between the American protocol and the British protocol. Kuppuswamy was in no state, mentally and physically, to participate in any talk on medical interventions.

Some semi-solid food was given to him. It tasted lousy, yet gave him some energy, which helped him co-operate more enthusiastically with the physiotherapist. Slowly, Kuppuswamy was able to walk with support all the way up to the nurses' station. He wished all the nurses a good day and thanked them profusely for all that they did when he was incapable.

One of the nurses asked him, "*Thatha*, do you not remember me from last time you were admitted? I am sorry, I should not have said that even in jest. *Meendum sandhikkumvarai, vidaiperuvathu Vanishree* (Till we meet again, bidding goodbye is Vanishree)."

It took Kuppuswamy quite some time to pacify her and convince her that her words meant no harm.

The day had started well for Kuppuswamy. It was nice to push some food down the throat. It was even more satisfying to see it remain inside for a while and get digested. He had a good undisturbed nap in the afternoon. Then he sat wide awake, waiting for the biopsy report. It would first appear online and only after the oncologists saw it, it would be printed for Kuppuswamy and his family to see. So the wait began for the panel of oncologists to come on their evening rounds, after they had seen the outpatients.

But before that, the much-awaited VIP arrived. Gas flowed first and then the bowels moved. And there it was. Soft stools that were not really loose. There was no pain, irritation or blood. It had come without prior intimation. Kuppuswamy knew only after the big job was done.

The uro-oncologist was all smiles when he walked in. "So the plumber has done his job right. And I have some good news too. We may not need any chemo, BCG or radiation for now, unless there is evidence of the cancer spreading elsewhere in the future. The biopsy has come in without any evidence of malignancy anywhere. It is time to celebrate," said the uro-oncologist.

Yes, indeed! They all had a tender coconut water party, along with the surgeon's wife who too was a doctor in the same hospital.

This was indeed a great relief as the very thought of a course of BCG sent a chill down Kuppuswamy's spine. He also didn't want to stay in Talgudi for too long. He was itching to get back home.

By the time it was day four, everyone was in a cheerful frame of mind.

"You need to get more and more mobile on your feet, for that is what will determine the date of discharge," said the surgeon.

The Foley catheter was removed and a urostomy bag with no extending tubes was fitted on the abdomen, thus making space for free movement. The stoma care nurse came to brief Kuppuswamy and his wife on the different types of appliances and the need for proper hygiene around the stoma: Dettol wash and tincture of Benzoin before each change.

The next four days saw a gradual recovery. There was an increase in Kuppuswamy's energy levels. Slowly, the smiles and the humor came back into the family. Kuppuswamy went for a walk three times a day easily. However, his request to go down to the ground floor for a *darshan* of the God at the temple below was turned down.

The rest of the stay in the hospital was uneventful. Soon discharge bells began to ring though the family was now getting a bit anxious about managing the stoma at home. Very soon it was day ten. "You can go home now," said the uro-onco-surgeon. That was at 8:45 in the morning.

As you can imagine what happens in a hospital, there were several formalities to be completed before they got the discharge summary and the surgical notes. The onco-registrar and the uro-registrar had to get together and draft the surgical procedures. Since the principal surgeon was busy in the outpatient department, the draft had to be taken to him there. After he was done with the outpatients, he made whatever changes he deemed necessary. Then the draft waited for the internal medicine department's approval. The doctor in-charge looked at it and detailed the current medication and immediate additional medication required post discharge.

The surgeon and the physician indicated the need for B12 and vitamin D supplements because a particular portion of the ileum was or was not used in constructing the conduit.

Kuppuswamy was happy to be leaving. The nursing staff were happy to see Kuppuswamy so cheerful. After all, he had made rapid strides on the road to good health.

The typist's duty began only at 10.30 a.m. By the time the discharge summary was typed, it was noon. A senior student then checked the draft and edited it on the computer itself. And when it was getting signed, the billing department was informed. But then it was lunch time.

The Kuppuswamys now understood the meaning of 'you can go now.' 'Now' meant 'in due course.' After lunch, the bill was prepared. Finally, at 2:45 p.m., Kuppuswamy's family was informed that the bill for four and a half lakhs rupees was ready for payment. Once this was done, it took another half an hour for a wheelchair and attendant to be free. Then they moved out of the room. It was only then that someone realized that the intravenous injection line was still on the wrist. This took another fifteen minutes for a nurse to come and remove it and the patient ID tag on the other wrist.

Finally, at 4 p.m., they were in the portico of the hospital. Soon they got into the car and reached home sweet home.

Poem - 3

You never realize I gave up my jaw
to that creeping crab, for you to enjoy the
smoke rings sent up like the cupid clouds
that is shown in the cartoons your son gleefully watches.

– **Arun M Sivakrishna** in *Songs of a Solitary Tree*

CHAPTER 8
THE HOMECOMING

Home sweet home

In the car, Kuppuswamy thought of all that had transpired in the last few days. He realized that medical intervention was a fine balancing act that involved taking decisions on the spot. Surgeons had a lot to contend with on the operating table. They had to make decisions regarding risk vs. benefit vs. quality of life. *Should we try preserving the bladder via BCG + chemotherapy + directed radiation doses? Or do we remove the bladder altogether? Then do we make an internal artificial bladder? The neo-bladder and self-catheter? What about the risks of infection? Or is it better to just get rid of the bladder et al and use an ileal diversion to a stoma into an external bag attached to the abdomen?*

The victorious warrior was home. He had the scars to prove. Not the surgical scars, for they were tiny, thanks to the robot. But they were the scars were from the missing bladder, the absent prostate, the diminished lymph nodes and most importantly the non-functional kidney with the ligated ureter. In their place, Kuppuswamy carried a urostomy bag with plenty of confidence. He cultivated a positive approach and looked forward to the days ahead. He would not simply exist but live, Kuppuswamy decided.

Kuppuswamy and his wife decided to stay in Talgudi till the quarterly review. When the family got down to reading the discharge summary, it dawned on them that the embargo on clopidogrel with aspirin, issued a week prior to the surgery, had not been officially lifted. This medicine had been prescribed after an episode of transient ischemic attack, a condition in which blood flow to the brain is temporarily blocked. It was a minor stroke, since it resolved on its own fairly quickly. Fortunately, a phone call to the attending physician in internal medicine resolved the issue and Clopilet-A was added to the current medication list.

Shortly after this, there was a phone call from a non-family-number. He was a dealer of, among other things, ostomy bags of various types for multifarious uses and all necessary accessories and appliances required by users of such bags, including the belt, wafer/flange, curved scissors, micro-tape, adhesive (stomahesive as it is called) and tincture of Benzoin. He wanted directions to reach Kuppuswamy's place and permission to come right away.

This was the new reality Kuppuswamy and his family would have to deal with.

Draining the ostomy bag accurately itself was a major task. The task of changing it frequently seemed a Herculean effort. The bag dealer helped Kuppuswamy with the changing that day. He also gave him detailed instructions and emailed a video for reference. He also warned Kuppuswamy that he would only supply appliances and not fit them in future.

Kuppuswamy practiced on a wooden plank, but finding a square of no wrinkles on himself was not easy. On bending, wrinkles appeared on the abdomen. These had to be filled or else the gap caused by it could be disastrous. So you had to find a small square space with minimum wrinkles. They also varied with your posture. If not done properly, the air gap could be a source of urine leak.

Apart from the issues of hygiene and embarrassment, this could lead to serious infections. The stoma and the skin in the immediate vicinity had to be meticulously cared for. A device had to be created to prevent the bag from getting wet during bath. If water seeped in, it would dissolve the adhesive and cause a yawning gap.

Soon it was time for dinner. Kuppuswamy waited with bated breath for home food after the bland ten-day regimen at the hospital under the dietician's directions. To be fair, the fault was not entirely with the hospital chef but with the attack of dysgeusia, a condition where the sense of taste and smell was distorted.

After dinner, Kuppuswamy had an undisturbed deep sleep. He slept without a care in the world, like a baby.

Next morning, everyone dear to him from near and far came to visit Kuppuswamy. They were absolutely delighted to see him come out of a surgery successfully, without any complications. His brother's family from New Zealand was the first to visit him. They had come to India for the preliminary arrangements of their son's wedding. They had migrated Down Under a long time ago. It was heart-wrenching to meet Kuppuswamy in such conditions.

Kuppuswamy was frail and fatigued and was barely able to walk across the room. He often stared at the ceiling wondering why he had come out of it alive. He seemed to be searching for the raison d'être of his continued existence.

"*Anna*, it is so painful to see you in this state. Please do buck up. There is a lot you need to do for us. We have almost finalized an alliance for Sudhir. The girl Sowmya studied in the same university as Sudhir. Her parents live here in India and the wedding will be held in Kerala," Kuppuswamy's brother, Kutty, began.

Kutty and his wife Kavi were very sad to see Kuppuswamy so ill. The very word 'cancer' had terrified them and indicated that he was seriously ill, even without knowing the exact details of the condition Kuppuswamy was in. As they learned more about his condition and the surgery, it was obvious to them that Kuppuswamy could not travel to Kerala to attend his nephew's wedding.

The family would sorely miss Kuppuswamy's cheerful presence as the groom's *periappa* but they knew it would be impossible for him to travel. So they accepted it calmly as God's will.

Suddenly Kuppuswamy's eyes brightened. A deeply buried source of energy seemed to have made its appearance. For a moment, he looked like the Kuppuswamy everyone knew.

"It will be nice if the wedding is held in Malgudi, for once I get back to Malgudi I won't be able to move out much, at least not in the immediate future."

Not wanting to dampen his brother's spontaneous and unexpected spurt of enthusiasm, Kutty said that he would certainly speak to the bride's parents and see if this could be worked out. On hearing this, Kuppuswamy was incredibly pleased. He then excused himself and went to bed.

Kadambini, Jagadeesh's wife from Alabama, and her two children were the next to arrive. The children were ecstatic. Her daughter displayed her Barbie dolls while her son showed Kuppuswamy his dinosaurs. The arrival of the children pulled Kuppuswamy out of the doldrums. With both Barbie and the dinosaurs vying for his attention, Kuppuswamy made the two fight one another. And like a child, he enjoyed the battle of Barbie versus dinosaur.

Kadambini's presence made it easier for Pramila to unload some of the burden she had been carrying alone all these months. It allowed her to leave her husband to the care of her daughter-in-law and go out for a while. A whiff of fresh air and some time spent at the mall (in small places even a supermarket was called a 'mall') brought the smile back on her face.

The exuberance of the children was indeed infectious. Both Kuppuswamy and Pramila enjoyed taking the children to the park nearby. The park had a path for walkers and a couple of swings, a see-saw and a slide for the children. While the kids played, Kuppuswamy took a walk on the path. And mother-in-law and daughter-in-law sat on a bench chatting about all things under the sun, except disease and hospitals. During one of their conversations, they both decided that Pramila needed a productive activity to divert her mind or else she could become miserable.

Pramila was the eldest of three daughters. She and her sisters had several discussions and came to the conclusion that it would be a good idea to open a boutique in Malgudi at an appropriate time. More on that later.

Days rolled by without any incident. Kuppuswamy's condition improvement gradually day by day. Soon it was time for the staple removal (from the suture) and the first post-surgery follow-up.

It was ninety days post-surgery. All the tests were taken. Though the tests came out clear with no recurrence or remnant of the tumor, another surgical intervention was required.

Among the tests performed for the review was a loopogram with contrast. This involved sending a dye through the stoma into the ileal conduit to track its flow up to the kidney. As it happened there was a block (constriction) somewhere inside and the dye was thrown back. Consequently, an ultrasound scan (also called ultrasonogram, abbreviated as USG or USS) was performed. First was a scan of the kidney, ureter and bladder (KUB) region and this was followed by a scan of the whole abdomen. These pictures showed that there was a blockage, most likely from some scarring effects, and hence the kidney was not getting fully voided and some urine always remained in the kidney. This condition is referred to as hydro ureteral-nephrosis or HUN in short. And when there is only one good kidney, such conditions are of vital concern. This requires correction by an interventional radiologist in a cath lab.

But the intervention could not be done immediately. Kuppuswamy was asked to stop taking Clopilet-A for five to seven days, before any surgical procedure could be undertaken, and then get admitted in the hospital the following week.

CHAPTER 9
HOSPITAL AGAIN

Antegrade stenting

The first quarterly follow-up required several tests to be performed before evaluation. The urologist wanted to know the amount of creatinine and urea in the blood as these two are the measures of efficiency of filtration by the kidneys. Blood tests for sodium (Na) and potassium (K) were needed by the internal medicine doctor, and the nephrologist was interested in the calcium (Ca) and phosphorous (P) levels in the blood. All of these were necessary to assess the various functions of the kidney and start with blood samples for testing and estimation.

Liver was one of the organs where the cancer was likely to have spread, and hence the monitoring involved measurements of liver functioning, again from blood samples.

Another likely site for metastasis (migration) was the lungs. So a regular chest x-ray was a routine requirement at all quarterly reviews.

These test results necessitated a referral to an interventional radiologist for guided PCN (percutaneous nephrostomy) insertion and antegrade stenting as a cath lab procedure. Kuppuswamy wanted to know what exactly this was.

Kuppuswamy was informed that a wire was going to be introduced from his lower back. The kidney would be punctured to flush out the stagnant urine. A protruding external stent would then be introduced.

He would be discharged the following day with two bags: one from the front for the stoma and another from the side.

After having discontinued Clopilet-A for five days, Kuppuswamy was back at the admissions desk of the hospital as early as 5 a.m.

Once he got to the fluoroscopy suite of the cath lab, it was a fairly straightforward procedure. Kuppuswamy was on conscious intravenous sedation. He was not knocked off completely but was rendered pain-free. He felt as though he was in a faraway tunnel and he could hear the conversation between the doctors from interventional radiology, nephrology and uro-oncology. He wasn't sure if they were actually there or the conversation was over a conference call.

Using ultrasound guidance, a one-shot puncture of the kidney's collection system was made. It was an exceedingly small puncture, less than 10 French or Fr (it is a unit of the outer diameter; 3 Fr is a millimeter). Hence, it would heal quickly. This was followed by a wire insertion and stenting was done. And then it was all over, except for refitting the urostomy bag.

This quick procedure was a contrast to the hectic radical cystoprostatectomy, barely three months ago. Both Mr and Mrs Kuppuswamy felt relieved. But their joy was short-lived. Kuppuswamy knew there was always light at the end of the tunnel, but he didn't know how long the tunnel was and when he would reach the end. After being discharged, he was asked to come back to the hospital in two weeks to remove the stent from the back and internalize it in the conduit with a double J stent. Kuppuswamy had heard of it. Some called it JJ and some called it DJ. He was not sure if they were one and the same.

So when he left the hospital, he did not feel liberated. He felt more like an accused out on bail.

With two bags to contend with, life was quite miserable. The discussion at home centered around what could have caused the constriction in the ileal conduit in the first place. The constriction or blockage in the ileal conduit did not allow all the urine to flow out. That was the reason for doing PCN in the cath lab. Often a new cancerous tumor developing in the area can cause the constriction.

Kuppuswamy contended that it could be due to some internal scarring. His family was worried if it was the tumor revisiting the site. Would it have shown on the ultrasound scan? Would urine cytology have helped clear the air? But would urine analysis done on urine stored in a plastic bag have given proper results? There were so many questions on everyone's mind.

Poem - 4

I am not a victim of cancer. I am experiencing cancer.
I am not dying. I am living.
I am not curing. I am healing and restoring.
I am not fearing. I am loving and trusting.
I am not fighting. I am ceasing all hostility and conflict.
I am not weak or diminished. I am strong and whole and complete.
My body is not my enemy. My body is my loving friend, my gentle guide.
My life story is not history. My life story is legendary.

– **Laura Barnes** in *Familyfriendpoems.com*

CHAPTER 10
HOSPITAL YET AGAIN

Internalization of the stent

The Talgudi *vaasam* (stay) was coming to an end. The thought of going back to Malgudi soon caused a spurt in the energy levels of everyone. The family soon got down to winding up things in the house. The house owner was informed over e-mail that they would be vacating the house soon, much to his chagrin. The domestic help was also told that her services would not be required much longer. All the hired appliances were returned. They also arranged a vehicle to transport all the furniture and kitchen appliances to be returned to the relatives who had parted with them when the Kuppuswamys were setting up their house in Talgudi.

The war against cancer was nearing its end. Bladder carcinoma had been conquered by Kuppuswamy with the help and support of an army of oncologists, urologists, nephrologists, anesthetists, cardiologists, neurologists and foot warriors such as the pathologists, dieticians, nurses, technicians, housekeepers, floor managers and other administrative staff. Thanks to the grace of God, the battle had been won without chemo and radiation. Kuppuswamy hoped the next quarterly review would put an end to everything.

In the midst of winding up, someone remembered that the PCN antegrade device had to be removed the next day. The ureteral DJ stent would then be internalized. The Kuppuswamys had one more small hurdle to cross.

Meanwhile, back in Malgudi, everyone was preparing for Kuppuswamy's glorious return, much like how Ayodhya geared up to welcome their hero Rama. There was happiness everywhere.

The next day, Kuppuswamy was back on the hospital bed. Since it was a quick and minor procedure, he was able to get the first slot in the day, just before daybreak. Soon it was time for general anesthesia again. Kuppuswamy was familiar with the anesthesiologist, who had graduated in Birmingham, UK, a year ago. She still carried the British twang as she exchanged pleasantries with Kuppuswamy. She engaged in small talk with him as she spoke about getting used to Indian hospital protocol.

Kuppuswamy knew that a conduitoscopy involving ureteric dilation and a double J stent insertion would be performed on him. Soon he became unconscious under the influence of anesthesia. A wire was passed from the nephrostomy into the ileal conduit. The dilation was up to about 12 Fr. A one-year stent was inserted. The position of the stent was checked and when it was found to be satisfactory, Kuppuswamy was moved to the recovery room. Soon he was out. He was relieved that the antegrade stent had been removed and he ceased to resemble Hanumanji with a tail of a stent hanging behind.

And like students rejoicing the end of their term, he recited, "No more English, no more French,

no more sitting on the old hard bench."

Kuppuswamy knew that doctors were not God. And patients and their near and dear were not the incarnations of the devil like some doctors believed. The robot that assisted in the surgery was not a surgeon. It was just a slave that carried out its master's instructions implicitly. The robot was just an instrument or tool in the hands of the surgeon.

Every doctor tried to be true to his profession, though a few accidents happened. These accidents were exceptions. Kupppuswamy believed all doctors acted according to the best of their knowledge and in good faith. Neither the specter of failure nor the ecstasy of success went entirely to them. Everything was a team effort. The doctors and his team members merely carried out the wishes of God.

The Kuppuswamys did not believe in blaming the doctors if anything went wrong. They were clear that if anything turned out to be less than perfect in the months ahead, it was not the surgeon who was to be faulted. No surgeon ever wished that his patients come back to him. The Kuppuswamys trusted their doctors and hoped for the best. And God was above all of them.

After expressing their gratitude to the medical fraternity in the hospital, Kuppuswamy and his wife paid a visit to a famous temple in the neighborhood. They had always wanted to visit the Guruvayoorappan temple in Guruvayoor but were too scared to venture out that far at that time. But they were happy when they heard that there was a Guruvayoorappan temple in the outskirts of Talgudi.

This was Kuppuswamy's first outing in a long time, the trips to path labs, loopogram centers, hospital OTs and cath labs notwithstanding. They went to the temple to offer a *thulabharam* as was the custom. They felt peaceful for the first time in a long time. All fears and worries gradually vanished.

The main deity in the temple, built using the Kerala style of architecture, was similar to the deity in Guruvayoor. The goddess Sri Bhagavathi Amman, representing the trinity Mahalakshmi, Saraswati, and Durga, was housed in a separate shrine. Kuppuswamy and Pramila offered a garland of bangles to the goddess before the *thulabharam* offer (the custom involves placing a person on one side of a balance and filling the other side with offerings such as coconuts or bananas till the scales are even). They also paid respects to Lord Venkateswara in another shrine.

Every day at eight in the morning and again at eight in the evening, the lord was taken in a small chariot to all the eight quarters of the temple. Just like in Guruvayoor, the outer walls of the sanctum sanctorum were adorned with brass lamps.

After propitiating the gods, the Kuppuswamys embarked on a seven-hour drive back home in the hired Xylo car.

Though tiring, there were no problems during the journey back home. They took two breaks at intervals of two-and-a-half hours each. Since they had left the temple early, they had not eaten anything. So the first stop was at a good hotel for a lavish south Indian buffet breakfast of *idli*, *vada*, *pongal*, *puri* and *dosa*, apart from corn flakes, bread with butter and jam, cut fruits, two types of juices and, of course, coffee. Kuppuswamy was delighted to find out that senior citizens had a forty per cent discount.

It was a great return home to Malgudi after four months of surgical intervention for Mr and Mrs Kuppuswamy. Suddenly everything seemed so bright and beautiful to them.

And when they reached home, Pramila's nonagenarian mother was delighted to see her son-in-law. It seemed as though she was holding on to dear life just to see him.

Kuppuswamy's mother-in-law was all tears to see her daughter's husband back from the clutches of the usually fatal (in her perception at least) disease. She kept talking endlessly until her throat ran dry. Then she asked for some *nimbupaani* (lemon juice). Soon after, she left for her house. Kuppuswamy would not meet her again, as the old lady succumbed to multiple massive cardiac infarctions in the middle of the night the very next day. It was as though she had made a personal pact with the Lord of Death, Yama, to keep her alive till she saw her son-in-law. And once that was done, her mission on earth was accomplished. She left without too much pain. Though she was admitted in the intensive coronary care unit at ten in the night, she didn't survive to see the sunrise again. She passed away peacefully.

There was no respite for Pramila as she had to look after her weak, surgery-ravaged husband on the one hand and take care of the arrangements of the last rites of her mother on the other. Since she had no brother, she had to shoulder all the responsibility being the eldest of three girls.

Soon a fortnight passed in no time.

CHAPTER 11
LIFESTYLE CHANGES

The trapped stent debris

The sudden turn of events did not cause any major discomfort to Kuppuswamy, who was kept away from everything and was called upon only when needed.

Kuppuswamy had enough things to contend with. The need to drain his urostomy bag every three hours was a little embarrassing initially. Also, every time he climbed the steep stairs, there was some trauma to the stoma, leading to the shedding of a few drops of blood. The urine discharge was yellow (it wasn't pale) and reminded Pramila of the need to make him drink more fluids. The doctors had advised that Kuppuswamy be constantly hydrated a wee bit more than normal people. The color of urine would be a very pale and almost transparent yellow if properly hydrated.

Kuppuswamy's appetite was almost normal, though he couldn't be fed a lot in one go. His food had to be spread across four sessions instead of three. Every time he ate, he seemed to get full too soon, only to get hungry again quickly. He flitted between states of 'hunger' and 'satiated' in quick succession. He was also feeling constantly dehydrated. He could only manage to consume two liters a day, whereas the mandate was three liters.

The bladder played a role in hydration apart from being a storage tank. In the absence of a bladder, continuous hydration was of paramount importance.

Kuppuswamy still suffered from dysgeusia. It remained a mystery to him as to why the condition was still strong. The hotter the food was, the more unpleasant was the odor from it.

Six weeks had elapsed since returning home. The urge to visit the family deity became stronger by the day. Normally, Kuppuswamy left before six in the morning and returned home just in time for lunch late in the afternoon. But now such a journey could turn out to be very strenuous. So Kuppuswamy had to think of an alternative plan.

Kuppuswamy booked a room in a good hotel at a walking distance from the temple entrance. He and his wife set off at 3 p.m. and reached the hotel around 5:30 p.m. They checked in and took some rest, after draining the urostomy bag. Then they had snacks and coffee, before leaving for the temple at 6:30 p.m. The *archanai* (offering) was made.

Then they got back to the room for dinner and sleep. Early next morning, they set off to the temple for more rituals. Then they got back to the hotel and checked out. They got back home after a three-hour ride. By spreading the journey across two days, they managed to have a good *darshan* of the deity with minimal discomfort.

However, this trip established the theory that Kuppuswamy could not undertake long journeys for the moment. He was in no position to attend his nephew's wedding in Kerala. He would also have to skip another wedding in Mumbai later that year. He decided to bless the married couples from afar.

All this made him wonder if life was worth living at all. He questioned the raison d'être of his continued existence. Pramila too appeared to be lost in a dark world of her own. She was no longer the cheerful woman that she had once been. She seemed to have withdrawn into a shell. If they had to get back to normal, they needed a diversion in life.

Pramila had been thinking of this for long. In fact, she had discussed it with her sisters too. Pramila felt it was time to open a boutique for women's clothes, accessories and gifts. She had an eye for such things and knew she would enjoy running a boutique along with her sisters.

They got going with the idea. Everything fell in place quickly. A place was finalized and the interiors were completed in record time. Soon it was time for the inauguration of the showroom. The Mayor of the Malgudi Municipal Corporation accepted their invitation to open the boutique. Several doctors and their families and the faculty of the Malgudi Medical College graced the occasion. They had a good first day with decent sales.

Amid the excitement of the boutique, Kuppuswamy forgot the burden of his demanding lifestyle. He assumed charge as the Chief Financial Officer of the company; the number work kept him engaged through the day. Whenever he felt low, he spoke to a few patients with a similar condition; they had been referred to by his oncologist. They cleared all his doubts and also gave him emotional support. Slowly, an idea was sown in his head. He wondered if he could pen all his thoughts and experiences into a book. It could serve as public awareness material too. But Kuppuswamy was afraid he would make medical blunders. After all, he was a nuclear physicist and was not too familiar with medical terms and surgical procedures. He did not want to complicate matters by relying on Google. He believed 'googling' medical conditions was the biggest blunder made by patients. But the idea was too powerful in his head to ignore. So he decided to write a draft and put it up on Facebook for senior doctors, medical students and surgeons to view and give their suggestions and corrections as he proceeded with the narrative. As he began writing, he felt renewed vigor. The draft had many enthusiastic followers from the medical fraternity who enthusiastically offered their inputs and cleared his doubts.

As for Pramila, she was enjoying her stint as the owner of a boutique. She took personal interest in procuring the products and training the sales girls. Soon the store came to be ranked high for customer service in the town.

As the days rolled by, the Kuppuswamys were due for another visit to the hospital. An SMS from the urology registrar reminded them that they had to get back to the doctor to review the stent. As encrustation of the stent was a possibility, it had to be changed.

The registrar explained that it was a very simple day-care procedure, but considering Kuppuswamy's age, he had to be admitted in hospital the day before for quarterly review tests including blood work, scan and x-ray to monitor metastasis.

The Kuppuswamys made an appointment with the surgeon, booked a room and also paid an advance for a one-hour slot in the OT. Soon Kuppuswamy was back on the hospital bed. He felt like a student taking a qualifying test for foreign medical graduates for the umpteenth time. The same question and answer session began.

"Sir, do you have sugar?" began the nurse.

Having been on the circuit for long enough, Kuppuswamy was in a jolly mode. This was a good sign as it would keep his stress-induced pre-surgery blood sugar elevations (hyperglycemia) away.

"No, I didn't bring any. I shall ask my wife to go home and bring it now itself. No one told me that I should bring my own sugar," joked Kuppuswamy. The nurse laughed and soon her interview ended. The stent review was scheduled for the morning.

It was not clear why, but the day always began very early in hospitals. Probably there were several tasks that the night shift staff had to complete before they handed charge to the day staff. Today was no exception. Soon it was time for the stretcher ride to the OT.

"Is this the TURP (prostate) case or the TURBT (bladder)?" asked a nurse. "No sister, I think this is the conduitoscopy," said another nurse. Kuppuswamy then explained that he was there for a stent change. The nurse assumed that it was the cardiovascular stent and told him that it was scheduled only for 10 a.m. So Kuppuswamy had to patiently explain to her that he was talking about the ureteral stent. Then the nurse confirmed that the uro-surgeon had arrived and was on his rounds.

And then it began. Kuppuswamy was placed in the lithotomy position (similar to childbirth) and given local anesthesia. The urethroscopy was done first and there was no evidence of recurrence of any tumor-like growth.

Then it was time for the conduitoscopy. The ileo-ureteral orifice showed the DJ stent in place with a stricture. Stent removal was attempted under the C-arm guidance, but the ureteroscopic removal of the upper end of coil retained in the ureter failed, as the surgeon was unable to negotiate across the spine. There was a bit of the stent debris still inside. The appropriate tools were unavailable at the hospital back then, Kuppuswamy was later told. Soon another double J stent was inserted.

Kuppuswamy was discharged later in the day.

The doctor then came to his room and announced, "Flexible ureteroscopic stent debris removal is being planned for the next quarterly visit in the main multi-specialty hospital." Kuppuswamy hoped that this hospital had all the necessary implements.

Kuppuswamy had his children by his side then. Arvind was the first to ask, "What is the bit of the old stent stuck inside likely to do?"

The doctor replied, "Literally nothing!"

Jagadeesh then asked, "Is it fixed or free-floating?"

"A bit of both, but it will stay at the pelvis."

"Can it bruise the walls and manifest itself in a sort of mild hematuria or occasional pinkish spotting?" asked Jagadeesh.

"Yes it can, but only very occasionally."

"Does it block or aid the smooth and rapid flow of the fluid, acting as a second stent?"

"No, it will not act as a second stent."

"What are the chances of reflux?"

"No chance of reflux."

"Does it cause the whitish mucus that appears with the urine to increase?"

"The mucus is because of the ileal conduit; it will not be affected by the redundant stent bit."

"How about hardening and clogging the outlet of the bag? Or will a blood clot sometimes do so?"

"Occasional blood would do it."

"Does it splinter by itself into smaller pieces and get scattered and then dissolve?"

"No, it cannot splinter, scatter or dissolve."

"Is another conduitoscopy the only way out?"

"Looks like it."

The game of suspicions began. The patient's near and dear questioned the medical team. The medicos pointed fingers at the hospital management for sub-standard stent purchases. The hospital management questioned the vendor selection committee. This committee asked what the quality assessment team was doing. After a lot of debating, Kuppuswamy and his family decided to drop the matter and leave it for the hospital's internal inquiry. Then they wondered if they had to change the surgeon or the hospital. Finally, they reconciled themselves to the fact that it was the act of God and there was no need for any change.

After the initial emotional cyclone passed over, calm was restored. All said and done, the team of doctors had toiled hard during Kuppuswamy's surgeries. Kuppuswamy owed his life to them. The doctors were younger than his own children and he couldn't blame any of them.

As they say, to err is human, to forgive is divine. Doctors may not be God, but patients did assume them to be divine.

Anyway, there was one more visit to the OT and Kuppuswamy hoped everything would be sorted out then. The Kuppuswamys had been to the hospital so many times that the security guards at the hospital believed them to be the employees of the hospital.

CHAPTER 12
THE BATTLE OF THE STENTS

The end of the war

It was supposed to be a very simple procedure, not very different from removing a Foley catheter and replacing it with another. Yet, to Pramila who was waiting outside the OT, in the antechamber nearby, those were tense moments. The OT was being guarded by a stern-looking grumpy security guard who always demanded money for tea. After what seemed like an eternity, though it was only an hour, two members of the surgical team came out and said, "We are so sorry. We couldn't remove the entire stent. A bit of it is still stuck inside. We do not have the proper instrument to handle it. We need a flexible URS, but we only have the rigid one. During your next visit, we shall do it at the main multi-specialty hospital where a flexible tool is available."

And that was that.

The Kuppuswamys were too shocked to react. But again, after the initial storm passed, they remembered the ninety-nine great things done by the medical team at the hospital. This was just one blip in the whole picture. They blamed it on the law of averages and decided to let it go. After all, it was only a bit of the ureteral stent. They forgave the unintentional error of the doctors, just like they would forgive their own children for petty mistakes.

Two months later, here they were back once again. Not at the same hospital but at the larger main multi-specialty hospital for removing the debris and re-stenting.

"Hi doctor. We do hope no complications arise this time," said Pramila, as soon as the uro-surgeon arrived.

"Once bitten, twice shy, isn't it?" the surgeon responded.

"I have a few doubts about the stent. First of all, are the stents inserted by cardiovascular surgeons for blood flow issues the same as the stents used in ureteral flow problems?"

"No madam, they are different because of the environment in which they reside."

"What material is the ureteral stent made of? Doesn't this material, as a foreign body, have to be compatible with the insides of the human body?"

"These stents are usually made of polyurethane, silicone or hydro gel."

"And doctor, do we get calciferous oxalates in or around the stent, in turn causing more constriction? Is this why the stents have to be frequently changed?"

"Encrusting does develop over the stents; that is why they are changed regularly."

"Would this show up on a USG of the abdomen?"

"On the USG, the stent shows up as a double line. On an x-ray, it is visible normally."

"Units of the size of stents, as also Foley catheters, are in the unit of F. What is this Fr unit?"

"A millimeter is equal to three French; the specification represents the outer diameter of the catheter and not the lumen."

"Thank you doctor. I am sure your patients and colleagues must be waiting for you inside."

In the OT, with the patient under general anesthesia, the surgeon, using a 22F cystoscope, saw a healthy lower end of the stent in the conduit. Flexible uretero-reno-scopic examination revealed the retained stent upper portion in the kidney.

The stent was removed using the rigid cystoscope as before. This time it slipped out easily. The guide wire was then pushed into the kidney. Then the access sheet was railroaded over it under guidance, till the left pelvic ureteric junction. The flexi ureteroscope was then manipulated up to the stent. The fragment and the other debris were retrieved in a basket. Next, a new DJ stent was deployed and the position was reconfirmed. Finally, the stoma was reapplied.

The stent and its debris were given to Pramila. And that marked the end of the ordeal. The hospital visits would now be fewer and far between.

Soon the Kuppuswamys started focusing on the boutique business they had started. They had a lot of fun. It was a new learning experience to procure and sell a wide variety of sarees from across the country—from the Surat sarees to the varieties from Central India. The sarees of West Bengal drew Kuppuswamy's attention immediately. The Manipuri silks also vied for his time. In a strategic move, the Kuppuswamys stayed away from local varieties and concentrated on sarees and dress materials from the northern states.

Business was not restricted to clothes alone. The boutique also retailed imitation jewelry from the artisans of Rajasthan and white metal gifts and utility items. The store soon became a landmark in the landscape of Malgudi.

Apart from procurement, Kuppuswamy was also engaged in maintaining the daily accounts of sales and the bank records. Since they had borrowed from a bank to purchase the initial stock for trade, the books had to be monitored constantly for debt liability. Commercial taxes required monthly filing of returns and VAT dues to be settled. Kuppuswamy also took charge of the hiring of the sales staff. Although Pramila and her two sisters took turns supervising the showroom, full-time sales girls were essential. The most taxing activity was marketing, promotion and advertising.

With so much work to be done at the boutique, Kuppuswamy had no time to be bitter about the past. He had put the past behind him. There was no turning back now. He was out of the tunnel. Kuppuswamy was no longer a cancer patient. He was now a cancer conqueror who was leading a perfectly normal life like any other person.

Yes, Kuppuswamy had conquered cancer, but old thoughts did sometimes invade the cancer conqueror.

Poem - 5

In hardship I became strong
battled until tumors gone
half the fight was in the mind
my pain was my cure

my great friends and family
gave me the strength to keep smiling
with their support, I survived
now each day's a thrill

— **Olive Eloisa Guillermo** in *Trembles and Thrills*

CHAPTER 13
THE SUPER SPECIALISTS

The astrologer and the medical tourism expert

Dr Ramanathan, son of an agriculturist, was a local boy who had scaled great heights. He was declared the topper at the Health Sciences University of Malgudi during the MBBS convocation ceremony. He later did a stint at the Alagappan Super Specialty Hospital in the state capital as a registrar in the Department of Uro-Oncology. But a genius cannot be entrapped in small confines and he soon found a large garden to flower at MD Anderson (MDA) in Texas. While he was there, this was the top cancer center in the US. It could have even been the best in the world.

There are far too many super-duper specialties in the spectrum of oncology. Cancer does not seem to spare any organ or node and often metastasizes in umpteen ways that are still unknown to man. There was so much to discover. But MDA could not quench Ramanathan's thirst. So he moved to Memorial Sloan Kettering (MSK) in New York City. MSK soon shot into top place in the rankings for cancer hospitals, pushing MDA to the second spot. Many say Ramanathan's exploits were primarily responsible for this.

This local boy was well versed in both the British (his bosses at Alagappan were British-trained vintage) and the American protocols. Now back in Malgudi, he had assembled a team of cancer specialists and equipment technicians to start a small oncology consultancy.

Ramanathan invited Kuppuswamy, a local hero who had conquered bladder carcinoma in situ, to address a session on modern post-surgery oncology management as part of the Continuing Medical Education program.

At the tea break, Kuppuswamy was astonished to note that all the doctors seemed ignorant of this new breed of 'super specialists' viz., medical tourism experts, who arranged everything according to a plan. They were always found loitering around the cafeteria, all suited and booted.

Kuppuswamy got into a reverie. In all hospitals during the outpatient consult, the surgeon issued to his patient an admit slip with instructions for the nursing station staff to execute on admission. With this, the patients booked a room or a bed in the ward. They also had to make an advance payment for the OT, as it was possible for the patient to suddenly disappear or go to another hospital in the big city. The patient and his entourage never went straight to the admissions desk. They converged at the cafeteria.

Over bakery items such as puffs, rolls and sandwiches and Kumbakonam degree coffee (if you were from the southern states) or samosas, shingda and tea (if you were from the North-East), patients pulled out a horoscope to be shown to the astrologer. Close by, on the side of the billing section, there was a photocopy machine to take copies of the numerous medical documents signed along with the surgeon's rubber stamp for insurance claims. Most people also photocopied the horoscope for astrological evaluation. Unlike the gigantic USGs, CT scans, MRIs, Carotid Doppler and blood work results that nobody ever really understood, everyone understood the twelve-box astrological chart. The astrologer always made sure you understood the static parts and the dynamic ones too.

Suddenly someone from the patient's group darted out. Ignoring the elevator, he raced up the steps to the second floor where the outpatient counters were located. A woman was yelling, "Tell doctor *sahib* that the OT is not available on that date. Free only in the midnight to 4 a.m. slot. Get him to endorse it for two days after that. *Panditji ke baare main math bathao. Samjhe naa, Sunil ka pappa.* They will simply laugh saying it is of no medical significance."

All medical indicators for an early resection vanished. The patient's organ would survive another day. And everyone praised the astrologer, their real super specialist, who extended the life of that organ.

Clinical research showed that a surgeon's errors were maximum in the midnight-to-dawn slot. So the surgeon simply rewrote the admit slip with the date desired by that patient on the advice of the astrologer. If the patient's request for an alternative date was not met, the patient would move to another hospital where the surgery could be performed on the desired date.

The cross-referencing between the astrologer and the medical tourism promoter irked all surgeons and hospital managements, but then this was the way of the world.

There was another super specialist in the hospital lounge opposite the pharmacy and beside the pathologist's sample collection chamber. He was the Medical Tourism Executive. He was ever ready to show around the hospital to anyone who cared to see. He took people on a tour of the cafeteria and parking lot as though it was a sight-seeing trip.

The medical tourism officer would say, "First let us see the big temple with the big bull before going to the big hospital. Today is *pradosham* day. So the big *abhishekam* starts at 4 p.m. Don't worry. Bruhadeeswarar and Brahanayaki will look after all your problems and the surgeon's too. The hospital admission desk is open *twenty-four hours. Anytime we can go there. This hospital is so nice. We don't charge for the toilet paper, mouthwash and palm sanitizer."

Parroting the oft repeated sentence "if you don't like the doctor or the hospital you are free to go elsewhere" could often be counterproductive. Options and alternatives existed even in small towns such as Malgudi and Talgudi.

Most hospitals reported quarterly financial guidelines based on 'captive' patients, and stock market traders played the futures and options on these numbers. Of course, it would require another chapter to elucidate the dilemmas of the patient who is also a dividend seeking shareholder of the hospital.

Meanwhile, on the second floor, an hour later, as the doctors stepped out of their cabins dodging the medical reps, one doctor was heard telling the other, "Guess what, that CIS bladder case, he wanted to shift the radical cystectomy by two days... Ask me why."

"*Bolo yaar, kyon aisa?*"

"Because his astrologer told him so. Even in this century, there are such... And we have to put up with them."

"*VIP patient ho tho aisa hi hoga.*"

"Ram, Ram *doctor ko khuda bachayen*. May God save the doctor."

And with these thoughts, Kuppuswamy suddenly woke up from his reverie to hear the session Chairman announce, "That was the most illuminating session we have had. And before the radiation oncologists take over, let us break for lunch."

Kuppuswamy used this opportunity to remind Dr Ramanathan to come home for dinner one day. He then rushed to the rest room to complete the draining ceremony. After which it was time to hail a cab and get back home.

As he sat in the cab, thoughts continued to invade his mind. And these thoughts moved from the past and quickly coalesced with the present. Kuppuswamy drank most of the water from his bottle to keep himself sufficiently hydrated. Soon he got home.

Kuppuswamy had to go out soon for a walk. He had to walk at least twenty minutes in the morning and twenty minutes in the evening. This prevented constipation and kept the stool softeners at bay. His vitamin D levels had been alarmingly low during the previous review. An early evening walk before sunset would help with this.

There was a park nearby. It was called the *thatha-paati* park or the *naana-naani bageecha* (park for senior citizens). Kuppuswamy walked around the park slowly. He was no longer as brisk as he was two years ago, before the historic episode of gross hematuria took control. But he was glad he was still able to walk. He had such illuminating conversations with important personalities on the park bench. He had a meeting with one such important person that day. This was none other than the stoma care equipment dealer.

Over a telephone call in the morning, Kuppuswamy had specified the things to be brought: abdominal flange/wafers, urostomy bags, tube of stomadhesive paste, tincture of Benzoin, gauze square strips, micro-tape and other essential items. And while he waited, Kuppuswamy's thoughts kept invading his mind.

Kuppuswamy wondered if he could have averted this situation by not smoking like a chimney in his younger days. Had he known that he would be sitting in a park waiting for urostomy bags, minus the bladder, prostate and several lymph nodes, he probably would not have smoked all those cigarettes with such relish and misconceived pleasure. Was all the secret smoking, scheming and strategizing worth it in the end? Did the teenage boys and girls he saw behind the tree in the corner of the park, puffing smoke away, know what they were getting themselves into? He had half a mind to display his abdomen, stoma and urostomy bag to them to deter them from smoking. But this could be deemed vulgar, thought Kuppuswamy.

He found immense satisfaction in the fact that the Juvenile Justice (Care and Protection of Children) Act, 2015 imposed a harsh penalty on the sale of tobacco to minors. The Act came into force on Friday, January 15, 2016. The Act recognized the harmful effects of tobacco and the tobacco industry's sinister design to specifically target vulnerable children. In a path breaking amendment to curb the growing menace of tobacco, the Act modified Section 77 as follows:

It is an offence against a child if a person gives or causes to be given to any child any intoxicating liquor or any narcotic drug or tobacco products or psychotropic substance, except on the order

of a duly qualified medical practitioner; shall be punishable with rigorous imprisonment for a term which may extend up to seven years and shall also be liable to a fine which may extend up to one lakh rupees.

Many more thoughts continue to invade the cancer conqueror even today.

REVIEWS

Prepublication Review - 1

Dr. Philip Jason, Senior Asst Professor of Urology, Chennai
December 27, 2015

"When Thoughts Invade the Cancer Conqueror" has been an exhilarating and thought-provoking journey, not just for our hero, Mr Kuppuswamy, but also for many of the doctors, who are part of this Facebook Group as well. Insights into a patient's pattern of thinking, his insecurities, grievances, hurt pride, bitter and sweet experiences, and doubts from a patient's perspective, have been an enriching feedback for me, and I am better for this journey, being a fellow - traveller with Mr Kuppuswamy on this ride; and I think most doctors of this Group would agree.

Prepublication Review - 2

Dr. A C Senthil Kumar, Consultant Surgical Oncologist, Chennai
February 13, 2016

It has indeed been an illuminating path, the journey of Kuppuswamy described eloquently in *"When Thoughts Invade the Cancer Conqueror."* The entire sequence from diagnosis of the feared C-lettered word, cancer, to the ultimate C-word, conqueror, has been indeed a great experience. It gives a nice insight into the way a patient, his family, and friends see the fight too. The moments of emotion ranging from despair, depression, joy, relief, hesitancy, guilt and shame. It indeed has been a rollercoaster. Kudos to Mr Kuppuswamy and his wife, Pramila, in wading through rough waters. Let the story of this conqueror inspire a thousand more Kuppuswamys.

Prepublication Review - 3

Dr N Venkatesh, Consultant Nephrologist, Chennai
February 14, 2016

Cancer! A word that often evokes silence, a loss for words, a veritable death sentence in the public mind. Is it possible to conquer it? Yes, indeed! But what it entails is a journey of pain, anger, loneliness, utter desperation followed by the triumph of the human spirit and love of man! Kuppuswamy's journey evokes all of these elements in a way that appeals to even the hardier doctors, who often force themselves to hide their anguish behind impenetrable exteriors as they go about Kuppuswamy's fight.

This book, *"When Thoughts Invade the Cancer Conqueror"*, is about all of these, the conqueror, his doctors, his relations that watch in silent desperation as their loved one walks down the valley of death all alone with only the blue-gowned angels for company! Kuppusamy's story is telling in its celebration of what man can achieve when conjugal love, science and providence can walk hand in hand. A truly inspiring tale of grit, spousal love, misunderstandings, disappointments, pain and the eventual conquest of a foe that can sap the spirit and kill the body. Kuppuswamy's tale truly is that of a conqueror, not of lands or kingdoms but of people and their common aspirations and above all what it means to be human. A must read for all those involved in the care and conquest of cancer.

Prepublication Review - 4

Dr. Amit Chaudhary, Senior Resident,·
Cardio-Vascular & Thoracic Surgery, Lucknow.
February 14, 2016

I heartfully congratulate the hero of this story, Kuppuswamy, for his perseverance, patience, and firm determination to fight with cancer and coming out as a winner. Final diagnosis can be anything depending on a battery of test, but most of us never ever felt the agony and pain a patient goes through because of uncertainty. It's a battle which only patient and his relatives fight once the concrete. Diagnosis of cancer is made. Kuppuswamy, the hero of "*When Thoughts Invade the Cancer Conqueror*" and Pramila, his wife are sources of inspiration to us doctors as also to many, many patients.

Prepublication Review - 5

Dr Maneesh Unnithan, Consultant Physician, Kozhencherry, Kerala
February 14, 2016

The book, "*When Thoughts Invade the Cancer Conqueror*", is an encouraging read about the events in the life of a cancer conqueror. Usually, we hear this kind of stories from our side, i.e, the doctor's point of view. It is a refreshing change that we are able to get a narrative so encouraging and emotionally overwhelming from a real cancer conqueror's perspective. I wish the authors all success in this venture.

Prepublication Review - 6

Arun M Sivakrishna, Mangalore.
Poet. Author of "Songs Of A Solitary Tree"
February 15, 2016..

Having had firsthand experience in the devastating effects, such a hurricane leaves in our lives; (we lost Dad to the abysmal depths this dreaded disease spirals people down), I always look up to people who had matched it ball by ball and pawn to pawn. The key is in believing yourself to be a Conqueror rather than just a meek Survivor. "When Thoughts Invade the Cancer Conqueror" is a conqueror's memoirs, one that deals in all its detail, the multiple fronts Kuppuswamy had opened up to send an enemy packing and like all brave soldiers, he too has scars and marks, medals and medallions. A war well fought.

It is an account of his trials and travails and the many sacrifices his family had to endure through different stages of surgery. It is a chronicle heralding the healthcare professionals, the technological advances in Oncology and above all, it gives hope to the millions that cancer is not a one-way ticket to hell, but a vindicating proof, that every journey does have a return ticket. I wish the authors all the best.

Prepublication Review - 7

Mrs Shobhana Krishnamoorthy, Nadanjali, Trivandrum
February 15, 2016

"When Thoughts Invade the Cancer Conqueror"; is an eye opener for the stranded ones to quit the habit, a story that throws light on the reality of the fight, an unending source of strength for those who are fighting the battle against cancer. With prayers to the Almighty for all those brave fighters. Wish the authors all the best.

Prepublication Review - 8

Mr S Krishna Kumar, VP(Finance), Mumbai
Actor, Prolific writer, and social activist,
February 15, 2016

The efforts put in by Sivaram (Nilakanta Siva) and Poorna(Rajalakshmi Siva) in bringing out this book, narrating completely from stage one through the path of hospitalization and several stages of surgery to the ultimate stage of complete recovery are indeed laudable.! "**When Thoughts Invade the Cancer Conqueror**" is about a patient's journey through Cancer –written, "with empathy and passion", about " a model patient –rational, considerate and above all a brave-heart. An apt read for families & patients dealing with Cancer –plenty of practical tips to deal with the mental, physical & emotional aspects ."

If after reading the book, even a few persons diagnosed with the big "C", can face life with a smile on the face and with a song in the heart, or if a family's spirits can be uplifted or if someone would begin to LIVE LIFE & NOT JUST EXIST…..the authors can consider themselves truly blessed to have been of some use to them. Wish the authors all success in the launch of this book which will be a "torchbearer " of the society.

Prepublication Review - 9

Mrs Geetha Paniker, Chennai, author of
When I fell in Love with Life - musings of a cancer survivor
February 16, 2016.

The experiences and anecdotes of Kuppuswamy reveal a daily battle and a take on life looking at the fear on its face and saying "I am not your victim." Turning your back and running away is the easiest escape, but in *"When thoughts Invade the Cancer Conqueror"*, Kuppuswamy gives us an insight not only to his battle with the emperor of maladies but also of what to expect and how to conquer it. An encouraging and inspiring journey of his battle with the odds against cancer, surviving it and then challenging it with a smile. This book takes us on a guided tour through the dreaded disease, how it was overcome through sheer perseverance to become a conqueror. Wishing the authors success in this venture too.

Prepublication Review - 10

Dr. A Arun Sundar, Asst Professor of Anesthesiology Villupuram
February 16, 2016

This book by Sivaram (Mr Nilakanta Siva) and Poorna (Mrs Rajalakshmi Siva) is a true inspiration to mankind. Their work is based on their personal experience combined with their enthusiasm and dedication to put forth a quality book with a lot of medical facts on a cancer conqueror's story looked upon from the point of view of the patient and his caregiver. I'm sure this is a real treasure and a must for every patient suffering from malignancy and those entrusted with their care. I am immensely impressed by their hard work, enthusiasm and dedication. Every word reflects their motive for an uncompromised work. Best wishes to both of them. I will recommend *"When Thoughts Invade the Cancer Conqueror"* to all my cancer conquerors who can read English.

Prepublication Review - 11

Dr. Sri Hari Singaram, Senior Asst Professor of Surgery Tiruchirapalli
February 17, 2016

The book, ***"When Thoughts Invade the Cancer Conqueror"*** written by patient and caregiver who turned authors chronicling the events of his disease and his thoughts while on treatment and thereafter, is an excellent reading for the doctors who treat the patient only as an object with repair in their garage. The dilemmas of the patient that need to be addressed before the treatment are best noted in this book. The survivor has made it a point that Cancer can be Conquered if not vanquished, though!.

Prepublication Review - 12

Mrs Sumathy Mohan, Homemaker, Navi Mumbai.
Tamil drama stage artiste and daughter of Cancer victim
February 17, 2016...

To present one's ordeal in the form of a story is indeed a unique way. For those who are suffering from Bladder Cancer, this will give some hope. As the authors, SIVARAM (Nilakanta Siva) and POORNA (Rajalakshmi Siva) have explained the treatment procedure and also explained most of the Latin, and Greek of medical terms hope they would have got answers, at least, to some of their doubts. Of late smoking is rampant not only among young men but also young women. Women's lib is one thing but they need not show their equality to another gender in this bad habit. May God save them. Hope this book steers them away from this undesirable habit.

Prepublication Review - 13

Dr. Laxmi Sankaran. Editor and Co-founder,
biotechinasia.com, *Singapore*
February 18, 2016...

It's not often that you meet someone who speaks about his tryst with cancer in such an objective manner, laced with wit and introspection. After a brief flashback, we get to the part where Kuppuswamy, is diagnosed with urinary bladder cancer. We can understand his agony when he reflects, "Wasn't a 15-year abstinence from burning tobacco sufficient atonement for the 40-year stint with it"? The support from doctors, family, his wife, the balmy words and moments with grand kids and his own grit help him fight the demon heads on and he does so with élan! From denial to acceptance to fighting the dreaded monster to becoming an entrepreneur, here is an inspiring story of a man who never gives up! Makes us re-evaluate our lives and gives some perspective!

Prepublication Review - 14

Mr Ramakrishnan Swami, Content Editor, Mangalore
February 19, 2016.

"When Thoughts invade the Cancer conqueror" is an achievement more than a mere effort on the part of the authors Nilakanta Siva and Rajalakshmi Siva. The thoughts of Kuppuswamy dipped in fear, anguish, surprise, and desperation - everything negative, brushed aside with sheer determination to come out of the lion's den, do provoke a sense of admiration towards the victim, whoever it may be.While reading this, I have felt sometimes that R.K Narayan himself has come out of his grave to say something more to the world!

I was a mute spectator to the sufferings of two "C" patients in my own family circles, Ignorance, and stupidity to keep the matter under lid were the main factors in those cases which went out of control leading to a painful ending. Let it not happen again and again, let us call a spade a spade, no more hush up, no more delay for prompt action.